ING
METAPHOR

Introducing Metaphor is an accessible introduction to the different ways in which metaphor permeates all areas of language, and other methods of communication, covering both theoretical and practical approaches to the analysis of texts.

Combining a variety of approaches to this widely studied subject, the book provides a thorough grounding in metaphor and word meaning, theories on the processing and understanding of metaphorical language, and metaphor in other languages and translation.

Knowles and Moon draw on a wide selection of authentic examples to explore metaphor in relation to text, discourse, and society. Metaphors are examined in a range of contexts such as politics, sport, and advertising, while literary metaphor is demonstrated through fiction and poetry. A final section covering non-verbal metaphor looks at metaphor in art, cinema, and music, further demonstrating metaphor theory in practice.

Featuring suggestions for further reading on topics in each chapter, and an appendix for small-scale research investigations into metaphor, *Introducing Metaphor* will be invaluable to undergraduate students of English Language, Linguistics, and Literature.

Murray Knowles and **Rosamund Moon** are lecturers in English at the University of Birmingham.

INTRODUCING
METAPHOR

*Murray Knowles and
Rosamund Moon*

Routledge
Taylor & Francis Group

LONDON AND NEW YORK

First published 2006
by Routledge
2 Park Square, Milton Park, Abingdon, Oxon OX14 4RN

Simultaneously published in the USA and Canada
by Routledge
270 Madison Ave, New York, NY 10016

Routledge is an imprint of the Taylor & Francis Group

© 2006 Murray Knowles and Rosamund Moon

Typeset in Perpetua by
Florence Production Ltd, Stoodleigh, Devon

1006175066

British Library Cataloguing in Publication Data
A catalogue record for this book is available from
the British Library

Library of Congress Cataloging in Publication Data
Moon, Rosamund.
    Introducing metaphor/Rosamund Moon and Murray Knowles.
        p. cm.
    Includes bibliographical references and index.
    1. Metaphor.   I. Knowles, Murray, 1948–.   II. Title.
    PN228.M4M66 2005
    808–dc22   2005006717

ISBN 0–415–27800–7 (hbk)
ISBN 0–415–27801–5 (pbk)

CONTENTS

ACKNOWLEDGEMENTS

There are many people who helped us as we wrote this book, and we are indebted to them all. We would like to thank in particular our families and friends for their constant encouragement and support; our colleagues at the University of Birmingham for their invaluable advice and interest; and our students, past and present, for their enthusiastic discussions of points and texts. We must also thank the (anonymous) reviewers of our manuscript: their suggestions and observations were greatly appreciated, and the shape of the final book owes much to them. Finally, we must thank Louisa Semlyen at Routledge and her colleagues Elizabeth Walker, Christabel Kirkpatrick, Kate Parker, Anne Robertson, and Julene Knox, who were all unfailingly patient, helpful, and positive at every stage.

Corpus data used in this book is drawn from the Bank of English corpus created by COBUILD at the University of Birmingham. Corpus citations are annotated as BoE.

The authors and publishers would like to thank the copyright holders for permission to reproduce extracts from the following:

A section of Chapter 8 was previously published in Murray Knowles and Kirsten Malmkjær (1996) *Language and Control in Children's Literature*, and is republished here, substantially unchanged, by permission of the publisher, Routledge, and its authors.

Extract from John Giles, 'Owen shouldn't be the scapegoat', from *Daily Mail*, 7 February 2003, © Associated Newspapers Ltd. Reproduced by permission of Solo Syndication.

Extracts from Rosie Gowan, Ireland correspondent, 'Peace process in turmoil after police raid Stormont', from *The Guardian*, 5 October 2002, © Guardian Newspapers Ltd. Reproduced with permission.

Extract from Mark Townsend, 'Alien invasion: the plants wrecking rural Britain', from *The Guardian*, 2 February 2003, © Guardian Newspapers Ltd. Reproduced with permission.

Excerpt from 'The Field Hospital' from *Poems: 1968–1998* by Paul Muldoon. © 2001 by Paul Muldoon. Reprinted by permission of Farrar, Straus and Giroux, LLC.

Text from Ariel advertisement reproduced by permission of Procter & Gamble UK.

Excerpt from 'Reconciliation' from *Collected Poems* by W.B. Yeats. © 1950 by W.B. Yeats. Reproduced by permission of A.P. Watt Ltd on behalf of Michael B. Yeats.

Every effort has been made to trace and contact copyright holders. The publishers would be pleased to hear from any copyright holders not acknowledged here so that this acknowledgements page may be amended at the earliest opportunity.

Murray Knowles
Rosamund Moon
February 2005

INTRODUCING
METAPHOR

To begin, the opening of a speech from *Hamlet*:

> To be, or not to be: that is the question:
> Whether 'tis nobler in the mind to suffer
> The slings and arrows of outrageous fortune,
> Or to take arms against a sea of troubles,
> And by opposing end them . . .

Knowing that this is a book about metaphor, you might, as you read through those lines, have picked out examples of figurative language: *the slings and arrows of outrageous fortune* or *a sea of troubles*, and the idea of taking arms, taking up weapons, against something intangible. Here now are the closing lines of Yeats's poem 'Byzantium':

> Marbles of the dancing floor
> Break bitter furies of complexity,
> Those images that yet
> Fresh images beget,
> That dolphin-torn, that gong-tormented sea.

The whole poem is packed densely with symbols and elaborate ideas, and here you might have picked out figurative language such as *bitter furies of complexity* or *that dolphin-torn, that gong-tormented sea*, or the idea of images 'begetting' other images. These kinds of creative, poetic, expression and idea are typical of literature, and it is literature with which metaphor is often associated.

But metaphor is not just a kind of artistic embellishment, at the rarefied end of linguistic usage, divorced and isolated from everyday communication. It is instead a basic phenomenon that occurs throughout the whole range of language activity. It is the intention of this book to introduce the study of metaphor and other kinds of figurative language, and to show how and why it is so important.

And, as you read that last paragraph, you might have noticed *its* metaphors: for example, *rarefied* and *divorced*. A typical context for *rarefied* is in relation to air which is less easy to breathe because of its distance above sea level (*rarefied* means 'less dense' or 'less solid'); and the typical context for *divorced* is in relation to the ending of marriages. We will come back later to the question of how we make sense of metaphors like these: for the time being, it is worth noting that 'divorced' might have different connotations for different people, according to their moral, religious, or political viewpoint. *Isolated*, too, could be classified as metaphorical, at least in terms of its etymology: it ultimately derives from a Latin word *insula* meaning 'island'. At a deeper, perhaps subconscious, level, we can identify a metaphorical conceptualization in phrases such as *at the . . . end of linguistic usage* and *occurs throughout the whole range of language activity*: here 'diversity' is represented, in some way, as if it had physical dimensions and existed in physical space. Finally, by referring to *the intention of this book*, we attributed our own intentions as authors to an inanimate object. This too is figurative.

ABOUT THIS BOOK

This book deals first with background and theoretical issues. In this first chapter, we will begin to define metaphor and to identify its different aspects, along with other kinds of figurative language, including metonymy. Chapter 2 looks at metaphor in relation to the meanings of words and phrases; Chapter 3 at systems of metaphor (some obvious, some operating subconsciously) and at how we conceptualize experience through them; and Chapter 4 looks at metonymy. Chapter 5 looks at models of how we understand metaphor, while Chapter 6 looks at crosslinguistic aspects of figurative language. Later chapters of this book take a different approach, and focus on figurative language in context. Chapter 7 considers evaluative and ideological aspects of metaphor in a range of social contexts; Chapter 8 considers literary metaphor; Chapter 9 considers non-verbal metaphor; and Chapter 10 rounds off by presenting some final examples. We give suggestions for what to read next at the end of each chapter, and suggestions for student research into aspects of figurative language in an appendix.

THE MEANING OF METAPHOR

Before going any further, we need to establish a working definition of **metaphor**. When we talk about metaphor, we mean the use of language to refer to something other than what it was originally applied to, or what it 'literally' means, in order to suggest some resemblance or make a connection between the two things. We can illustrate this with two examples taken from the Bank of English corpus (BoE), a 450-million-word corpus of recent English texts (see Chapter 5 for discussion of corpus linguistics and metaphor). In this case, they are metaphorical uses of single words or phrases, although metaphors can be developed over much longer stretches of text:

> The **jewel** in Northumbria's ecclesiastical **crown** is Lindisfarne Priory on Holy Island, built as a monastery in 635 and reached by a tidal causeway.

> We used to **thrash** all the teams in the Keith Schoolboy League. We had a great squad and no-one could **touch** us.

Clearly, a priory is not a jewel in the way that a diamond or sapphire is, nor does Northumbria have any sort of ceremonial headgear in the way that a monarch traditionally has: the literal meanings of *jewel* and *crown*. Clearly, one team is unlikely to have hit the other teams with sticks or whips, and equally unlikely is the impossibility of anyone making physical contact: the literal meanings of *thrash* and *touch*. We recognize these words in these contexts as exaggerations and non-literal, and we interpret them accordingly. *Jewel* represents something that is valuable, attractive, and desirable, and *a jewel in —'s crown* refers to the most important or valuable achievement; *thrash* suggests the totality of a victory, and *touch* suggests achievements and success which are much greater than others seem capable of.

This explanation of metaphor is of course dependent on a definition of literalness. Unless we identify and agree what the **literal** meaning of a word or expression is, we cannot identify and agree what is metaphorical. We will come back to defining literalness when we consider different kinds of figurative language later on in this chapter.

THE IMPORTANCE OF METAPHOR

Metaphor is pervasive in language, and there are two principal ways in which it is important.

First, in relation to individual words: metaphor is a basic process in the formation of words and word meanings. Concepts and meanings are **lexicalized**, or expressed in words, through metaphor. Many senses of multi-sense words are metaphors of different kinds, as in he meanings of *field*, *hurt*, and *dark* in the following BoE examples:

> She has published extensively in the **field** of psychology.

> The failure has **hurt** him deeply.

> . . . the end of a long tale, full of **dark** hints and unspeakable innuendos.

Similarly, the names of many new concepts or devices are metaphorical or extended uses of pre-existing words: for example, computer terms such as *web*, *bug*, and *virus*. Many compound words encapsulate metaphors: *browbeat*, *foothill*, *pigeonhole*. Idioms and proverbs are often metaphorical in origin: *don't put all your eggs in one basket*, *miss the boat*, *rattle someone's cage*, and, more obscurely, *kick the bucket* and *a red herring*. These are mainly **conventional** metaphors (see below), and we will discuss them further in Chapter 2.

Second, in relation to discourse: metaphor is important because of its functions – explaining, clarifying, describing, expressing, evaluating, entertaining. There are many reasons *why* we use metaphors in speech or writing: not least, because there is sometimes no other word to refer to a particular thing. But where we have a choice, we choose metaphors in order to communicate what we think or how we feel about something; to explain what a particular thing is like; to convey a meaning in a more interesting or creative way; or to do all of these. We will look at examples later. Significantly, a lot of our understanding of things is mediated through metaphor. That is, we might well not understand them except with the help of metaphorical models or analogies, and our understanding is itself conditioned by the metaphor. For example, the cells in our bodies react biologically in complex ways to infection: we can understand the process more easily through a metaphor of war, thinking of it in terms of fighting and invasion, as in

> Scientists believe stress may suppress development of T-cells, the white blood cells which help to **fight off invading** micro-organisms.
>
> (BoE)

Other metaphors might have been used, but this is the dominant, most familiar one, and the way in which we now conceptualize the biological process is determined by it. Similarly with the example *throughout the whole range*, from earlier in this chapter: we represent diversity as physical space. It is typical that metaphors use concrete images to convey something abstract, helping to communicate what is hard to explain.

CREATIVE AND CONVENTIONAL METAPHORS

We began this chapter with examples of literary language: with *the slings and arrows of outrageous fortune* and *that dolphin-torn, that gong-tormented sea*, Shakespeare and Yeats create poetic effects by creating new images. We informally described this kind of language as creative, but *creative* has a more technical meaning when applied to metaphor. **Creative metaphors** are those which a writer/speaker constructs to express a particular idea or feeling in a particular context, and which a reader/hearer needs to deconstruct or 'unpack' in order to understand what is meant. They are typically new (another term is **novel metaphor**), although they may be based on pre-existing ideas or images, such as a traditional representation of fortune as a person, whether enemy or friend. Creative metaphor is often associated with literature, but there are plenty of instances of it in other genres. Here are two taken from, respectively, a tourist guide and restaurant criticism, which we will return to later on:

> The main street follows a higgledy-piggledy contour from the safe, sandy cove beside which the east village sits, towards a busy harbour full of the rippled

reflections of brightly coloured fishing boats and **cradled by the crooked finger** of the harbour wall.

(Greenwood et al. *The Rough Guide to Ireland*, 1999: 227)

Got second Martini. No delicate shaving of lemon peel, just twisted to release oils, but two strips of thick peel bearing pith. And it was warm. Not **the silver bullet whistling through the rigging**, as it should be.

(Matthew Fort *The Guardian* (*Weekend*), 17 March 2001)

Creative metaphors contrast with **conventional metaphors**. These are metaphorical usages which are found again and again to refer to a particular thing. Cases in point are the metaphors of cells *fighting off* infection and of micro-organisms *invading*; and the metaphorical meanings of *divorced* to mean 'completely separated' and *field* to refer to a specialized subject or activity. These kinds of metaphor are institutionalized as part of the language. Much of the time we hardly notice them at all, and do not think of them as metaphorical when we use or encounter them: dictionaries are likely to record them as separate senses.

The term **dead metaphor** is sometimes used to refer to conventional metaphors, especially those which people do not recognize as metaphorical in ordinary usage. We will not use this term, but it can be found in many discussions of metaphor.

FIGURATIVE LANGUAGE: TERMS AND TYPES

So far, the metaphors mentioned have been of very different kinds, and it will already have become clear that the term metaphor itself covers several different linguistic phenomena. What they have in common is that they are non-literal, figurative uses of language. While metaphor is the best-known form of figurative language, there are others too. We now need to look at figurative language more widely, and to introduce simile and metonymy: we also need to define some terms more precisely.

We have used the term non-literal: but what is **literal**? How do we know or identify what the literal meanings of a word or utterance are? In the simplest cases, a word's literal meanings refer to a concrete entity – something with physical existence in the world – and its non-literal meanings refer to something abstract, or to abstract qualities.

Word	Literal meaning	Metaphorical meaning
fox	an animal	a cunning, wily person
jewel	an ornamental precious stone	something valuable
mountain	a large piece of rock/ground	a large amount of something

So the literal meaning here is the most basic and physical meaning: the meaning that is most likely to occur to us if we are asked to explain what the word means, out of context. The literal meaning is also typically the earliest historically: metaphor is a historical (or diachronic) process.

Metaphors, therefore, are instances of non-literal language that involve some kind of comparison or identification: if interpreted literally, they would be nonsensical, impossible, or untrue. The comparison in a metaphor is implicit. If we say that someone is a fox or that something is a jewel, we are comparing them to a fox or jewel, and mean that they have some of the qualities that are traditionally associated with foxes or jewels.

A subtype of metaphor is **personification**, where something inanimate is treated as if it has human qualities or is capable of human actions. In *to take arms against a sea of troubles*, troubles are personified as a human enemy – as is 'outrageous fortune'; similarly with the cells and micro-organisms in *the white blood cells which help to fight off invading micro-organisms*. Two further examples are

> 15 years later the company moved into the **friendly glass and brick building** in Wellington Circus, with its almost circular auditorium designed by Peter Moro.
>
> (BoE)

> The wind began to **scream**, and we could see **the tops of the long-leafed pine trees doing a mad dance** against the black sky.
>
> (BoE)

where it is, of course, not the building which is actually friendly, nor are the trees actually dancing; while verbs such as *scream*, *howl*, *whisper*, *shriek*, which more literally describe human or animal noises, are conventionally used metaphorically to describe the sound made by the wind, machines, or other inanimates. Personification as a kind of metaphorical transfer or anthropomorphism can be important, as we will see in Chapters 7 and 8.

Similes are very like metaphors, but there is one important difference: the comparison is explicit. That is, similes are introduced or signalled by words such as *like*, *as*, *compare*, *resemble*, and so on. To say that someone is a fox is to use a metaphor; to say that they are *like* a fox is to use a simile. There may appear to be little difference between the metaphor and the simile: just an arbitrary change of phraseology. However, there is an important philosophical distinction. A metaphor is literally impossible or untrue, and on the surface, metaphors are paradoxes or falsifications: after all, a person is a person and not a fox, however they behave. In contrast, a simile is literally possible or true, even if it is not especially appropriate or clear. We should add that some scholars regard the metaphor/simile distinction as more important than others do. The following examples of similes both emphasize speed and suddenness:

> Not just anxiety, but sheer panic seized them. They took off **like a bullet from a gun**.
>
> (BoE)

> There followed a chase in which we all ran **like rabbits**.
>
> (BoE)

The first also suggests forcefulness and purposefulness; the second, perhaps, vulnerability and desperation.

Simile is also the term for a type of fixed phrase that follows the pattern *as clear as crystal*, *as white as a sheet*, *as thin as a rake*, *as cheap as chips*.

Metonymy is an important kind of non-literal language. Broadly, cases of metonymy involve part-and-whole relations and associations. The word for a part of something is used to refer to the whole, or else the whole is referred to in terms of something associated with it. An example of the first type is *hand*, used to refer to a worker, especially a manual worker (*manual* itself comes from a Latin word meaning 'hand'): it also occurs as the second element in compounds such as *chargehand* and *farmhand*. The metonym draws on the body part of those workers that seems most relevant. Compare similar metonyms in other contexts: football commentators sometimes refer to a substitute player as *a fresh pair of legs*; and the emigration of top-ranking scientists, scholars, and thinkers is sometimes referred to as the *brain drain*. An example of the second type is *the stage*, used to refer to the theatrical profession and its activities.

While metaphors are literally impossible or untrue, metonyms are partially true. There is some observable, often physical, connection between the metonym and its meaning, whereas metaphors rely on comparisons of sorts. For this reason, many linguists distinguish carefully between metaphor and metonymy, seeing them as complementary but quite separate. Some, however, see metaphor as a form of metonymy, or having developed out of metonymy. Furthermore, individual phrases or stretches of figurative language can be both metaphorical and metonymic. We will look at metonymy in more detail in Chapter 4.

ANALYSING METAPHORS

To analyse and discuss metaphors in any depth, we need to identify and consider three things: the **metaphor** (a word, phrase, or longer stretch of language); its **meaning** (what it refers to metaphorically); and the **similarity** or **connection** between the two. In traditional approaches to metaphor, including literary metaphor, these three elements have been referred to as, respectively, **vehicle**, **topic**, and **grounds**. We can see how this works with the cases of *mountain* and *invade*.

context   Be prepared for a mountain of paperwork

metaphor/vehicle   mountain
meaning/topic   a large amount
connection/grounds   ideas of size, being immovable and difficult to deal with

context   ... the white blood cells which help to fight off invading micro-organisms

metaphor/vehicle   invading
meaning/topic   developing in ways and places that cause ill health
connection/grounds   idea of intrusion into places in harmful, dangerous, and unwanted ways

The **topic** of a metaphorical usage is its intended meaning, not its literal meaning (some writers use the term **tenor** rather than *topic*). When we analyse the **vehicles** of metaphors, it is the **grounds**, the relationship between the literal and metaphorical meanings, which provide the key to how effective that vehicle is: this applies both in the case of conventional metaphors (*fox*, *invade*, *mountain*) and highly creative ones (*that dolphin-torn, that gong-tormented sea*). By examining the grounds, we can see how the metaphor works: the special significance of the way in which meaning is being conveyed, and which particular features of the literal meaning of the vehicle are being transferred to the topic. For example, the conventional metaphor *mountain* exploits ideas of the size and immovability of mountains, but there are other features which might have been drawn on – prototypical mountains are cold, perhaps snow-capped, rocky, jagged or pointed, inhospitable, infertile. It is useful to consider which prototypical features are transferred and which are ignored or suppressed.

We can use this to analyse the metaphor in the description of the unpleasant Martini:

> Got second Martini. No delicate shaving of lemon peel, just twisted to release oils, but two strips of thick peel bearing pith. And it was warm. Not **the silver bullet whistling through the rigging**, as it should be.
>
> (Matthew Fort *The Guardian (Weekend)*, 17 March 2001)

The vehicle is *the silver bullet whistling through the rigging*, and the topic is the taste of an ideal Martini. For the grounds, we can see an analogy between the speed, forcefulness, and sudden explosiveness of the bullet, though not its potential destructiveness; and the coldness and dryness of the drink, along with the sudden sensation of its taste. We can compare the way in which the adjective *clean* could be applied to both topic and vehicle here: that is, it is used to describe flavours and smells on the one hand, and actions, including the firing of bullets, on the other. The metaphor crosses over between senses: an image based on sight and sound, and also touch, is applied to taste. This kind of crossover is sometimes referred to as **synesthesia**.

SYMBOLS AND METAPHOR

This book is about figurative language. Metaphors and metonyms are a form of symbolism, and it is possible to find non-verbal or non-linguistic metaphors and metonyms in media other than language: dance, music, and particularly visual media such as signage, art, and cinema and TV. For example, a slanting *Z* on a road sign metaphorically represents a double bend, while a knife and fork metonymically represent a café or restaurant. Classic cinema makes use of stock, conventionalized, metaphors and metonyms to represent events and feelings. For example, the metaphor of characters going off into a sunset at the end of a film is used to represent the rest of their lives, while storms or fogs are used not only as narrative devices but also metaphorically to represent emotional turmoil or mystery; metonyms such as bells pealing or tolling are used to represent weddings or death, and grazing animals to represent peaceful non-urban life. See Chapter 9 for discussion of non-verbal metaphors.

Many of the metaphors that we will look at will be words or phrases: few will be longer than a paragraph. However, it is possible to see whole texts as metaphorical: a story that concerns one set of events and people is really a metaphor for another. This, broadly, is what **allegory** is, with the metaphorical reading usually having moral significance. Think, for example, of Aesop's fables; stories such as *The Lord of the Rings*, or children's stories such as *The Princess and the Pea* or *Hansel and Gretel*; political novels such as *Animal Farm*; religious texts such as the parables in the Bible; and, non-linguistically, many paintings and other works of art.

THE FUNCTIONS OF METAPHOR

We will return in later chapters to the reasons which underlie the use of metaphor: metaphor has a purpose. As preliminary discussion, we can usefully begin with the non-verbal examples just mentioned. Why does a road sign have a slanting Z and not just the word *double bend* and why should film-makers end with characters riding off into the sunset, or include storm and fog scenes rather than verbal expressions of emotion or bewilderment? Perhaps because less is more: the visual impact of a stylized road sign is faster in terms of communication than that of words, passed at speed; and what is left unstated in a film is more resonant and leaves more to the imagination than what is said. We know what kind of thing is meant, or is going to happen, and we can fill in the gaps ourselves.

Something similar is true for linguistic metaphor, especially creative metaphor. By using metaphors, much more can be conveyed, through implication and connotation, than through straightforward, literal language. Take the case of *the silver bullet whistling through the rigging*: how could the writer have communicated his idea, in a non-metaphorical way, of what a perfect Martini should be like? Would this alternative wording have been as powerful a description, or as succinct? Or that literary metaphor *dolphin-torn*: what exactly is Yeats suggesting about the sea, and how else could this have been expressed? Just as writers convey meanings more open-endedly when they use metaphorical language, readers interpret less narrowly than they would literal language. So meaning is communicated between writer and reader in a less precise way, even though the metaphors may seem concrete and vivid. It is this imprecision, this 'fuzziness' of meaning, which makes metaphor such a powerful tool in the communication of emotion, evaluation, and explanation too.

Conventional metaphors may not seem to communicate in the same way as creative metaphors: their meanings are more fixed, and do not normally involve processes of implication by the writer and inference by the reader. But the metaphorical content is interesting nevertheless. The ideas, assumptions, and beliefs of a culture are present in its conventional metaphors, even if this is not apparent on the surface. One way to examine ideology is through metaphor, and we will begin to do this in Chapter 7. The next two chapters prepare for this by focusing on conventional metaphor.

FURTHER READING

This book is only an introduction to key issues in the study of metaphor and other forms of figurative language. A great deal has been written already on the subject, and further papers and books appear each year, presenting new ideas and sometimes revising earlier ideas. This means that it is important to take account of recent publications and new editions of earlier publications.

The following two books give general overviews of metaphor: we will give references for selected further reading on specific aspects of figurative language in later chapters.

Goatly, A. (1997) *The Language of Metaphors*, London: Routledge.

Kövecses, Z. (2002) *Metaphor: a Practical Introduction*, Oxford: Oxford University Press.

METAPHOR, WORDS, AND MEANINGS

In this chapter, we will look at metaphor in relation to the meanings of individual words and phrases. We will mainly be concerned with conventional metaphor here, rather than creative metaphor, and much of what we cover will be bound up with the histories of words, and the development of meanings over time. Historical aspects of metaphor are sometimes thought less interesting and relevant than textual aspects (such as the effects of metaphor on us as readers, and the kinds of complex meaning which are being conveyed). However, historical aspects help explain what metaphor is, how metaphors develop, and how they produce the effects and meanings that they do.

METAPHOR AND ETYMOLOGY

The following compound words all embody some kind of metaphor:

a **cooling-off** period . . .

freelance workers; to work **freelance**

to **green-light** a project

a **last-ditch** attempt . . .

pigeonholes; to **pigeonhole** someone

seed money

In each case, the metaphorical meaning is more usual than any literal meaning in current English. Although it is possible to have a literal 'cooling-off' period – perhaps a period of cooling down, after exercise or lying in the sun – the expression usually refers to a period after the signing of an agreement, when it is still possible to cancel it. 'Seed money' could be money for buying seeds, but usually refers to money that is loaned to an organization or group to enable them to start up a project. *Last-ditch* and *pigeonhole* can both be related to metaphors and visual images, and *freelance* is a metaphorical transfer from a mercenary knight, literally and originally someone with a lance who was 'free' or uncommitted.

Other words may not at first seem metaphorical; however, many have developed through metaphorical uses of their root words in Latin, Greek, and other languages. In Chapter 1, we mentioned that the word *isolated* derived from the Latin word *insula*, meaning 'island', and some further cases are:

ecstasy	from Greek *ekstasis*, 'standing outside oneself'
involve	from Latin *in* + *volvere*, 'in/into/inside' + 'roll'
kamikaze	from Japanese *kami* + *kaze*, 'divinity' + 'wind'
poppycock	from Dutch *pappekak*, 'soft dung'
sarcastic	from Greek *sarkazein*, 'speak bitterly', ultimately 'tear the flesh'
sullied	from French *souiller*, 'to soil'

The etymological roots may conjure up visual images, and suggest reasons why the words have their current English meanings.

Some information about the etymologies of words can be found in most large general dictionaries of English: more detailed information can be found in dictionaries of etymology or in historical dictionaries, of which by far the most important is the *Oxford English Dictionary* (*OED*).

METAPHOR AND POLYSEMY

Polysemy is the technical term for words with two or more senses. Dictionaries show that most common words in English have several senses, and many common words have a large number of senses which have developed over time. There are several ways in which senses develop from an original meaning, but very often they develop through figurative processes of metaphor and metonymy.

To take the word *branch*: what does it mean, and what image comes into our minds when we think of the word? We are most likely to think of the branch of a tree. However, we may visualize a branch that is attached to a tree, covered with green leaves or blossom, or maybe bare; or a branch of a pine-tree; or a branch of a fruit tree, laden with fruit; or a fallen branch, lying on the ground. Our friends and families may have the same images, or very different ones; however, it is probable that the first meaning of *branch* which occurs to us will be a woody part of a tree.

Most dictionaries give this 'tree' sense of *branch* first, as sense 1, but they are likely to list other senses of *branch*:

> a subsidiary road, railway, or stream, leading off a larger one
>
> a subsidiary office or place of business that is part of a larger organization (*a branch office; the local branch of a nationwide chain of stores*)
>
> a division or sub-area of study or learning (*branches of learning*)
>
> a sub-division of a family (*another branch of the family settled in Texas*)

and so on. Some dictionaries combine some of these senses; others keep them separate and add further technical senses to do with mathematics, computing, and physics. (Note that very few modern monolingual dictionaries label senses as metaphorical, even where the metaphoricity is clear.) There is also a verb *to branch*, which is commonly used to mean 'to go in a different direction', both literally and metaphorically, as in *the path branches off here* and *they decided to branch out on their own*.

The senses are now established and recur: it is not difficult to understand how they have developed, and what kinds of analogy have been drawn. If we look at them from a historical point of view, the *OED* records that the 'tree' sense of *branch* first appeared in English in the last part of the thirteenth century, and records several of these other senses as first appearing in the following two centuries. These metaphorical uses are old as well as common.

CORE MEANING, METAPHOR, AND FREQUENCY

Many polysemous words are like *branch*. They have a basic meaning which refers to something concrete or physical, from which have developed further senses which are often metaphorical. This basic meaning is sometimes referred to as the **core meaning**. Consider, for example, the following nouns, where there are fairly clear connections between core and metaphorical senses (contexts are taken from BoE):

> **cream**: . . . porridge was served with **cream** and brown sugar; . . . the **cream** of pop: Bono, Robbie Williams, the Manic Street Preachers . . .

> **fossil**: . . . he's found the **fossils** of two very small, very early birds; The old **fossils** were moaning they had yet to receive their lap-top computers.

> **stream**: . . . a country house in woodland with its own trout **stream**; . . . a small but steady **stream** of visitors.

A similar phenomenon is found in verbs where the core meaning refers to a physical activity or process, and adjectives where the core meaning refers to a physical quality. For example, the core meaning of *to feed* is 'to eat' or 'to give food to someone/something': metaphorical senses can be seen in contexts such as *feeding your imagination* or *feeding lines to an actor*. The core meaning of *hollow* is 'not solid, empty': metaphorical senses can be seen in contexts such as *their words rang hollow*, *it raised a hollow laugh*, and *a hollow victory*. Similarly with the following (contexts from BoE):

> **float**: A flotilla of tall ships **floating** along the Hudson river . . . ; . . . press releases **float** from office to office with compelling ideas but no practical plan for making them happen.

> **nail down**: Lay the roofing felt flat on the roof and **nail** it **down** using galvanised clout nails; . . . they have more work to do to **nail down** the connection between global warming, shifting cloud layers and ecological disruption.

> **juicy**: . . . ripe, **juicy** peaches . . . ; . . . all the latest news and **juicy** gossip from around the world.

> **magnetic**: . . . the curved force lines of the **magnetic** field . . . ; Foreign investment . . . is further proof of the city's **magnetic** attraction.

In many cases, the core meaning of a word is its oldest and most frequent sense. However, there are other cases where the oldest, literal sense is actually less frequent than a metaphorical one. In fact, sometimes the original concrete sense is now so rare or restricted in use that the sense which we think of first, or think of as the core meaning, is the metaphorical one. The original sense of *culture* related to the cultivation of plants and crops, but now the dominant sense relates to arts, learning, and other signifiers of civilizations, while the earlier sense is mainly restricted to scientific and horticultural contexts. Sometimes the original, literal sense has died out altogether: *muddle* originally meant 'wallow in mud' or 'make muddy', and *solve* originally meant 'loosen' or 'unbind'. The case of *impress* is more complex. Its dominant sense now is 'cause someone to have a favourable opinion', as in *it impressed me* and *I was very impressed by . . .*; its original, literal sense was 'apply pressure to, so as to leave a mark', and although now virtually obsolete, it can be traced in a current metaphorical sense 'make someone realize the importance of something', as in *they impressed upon me that . . . .* The related noun *impression* retains the original literal sense, 'indentation, mark', but the metaphorical sense 'reaction, opinion, idea' is considerably more frequent.

METAPHOR AND GRAMMATICAL WORDS

The words which we have been considering are lexical words; however, many grammatical words also have metaphorical uses, although it is less easy to discuss these in terms of core meaning and polysemy. Perhaps the most obviously metaphorical are prepositions and adverbs, where their first senses often seem to refer to physical position, direction, or extent – as far as it is possible to reconstruct the historical development of languages from the surviving text evidence. For example, the physical sense of *in* (*put it in a box*; *let them come in*) seems to be historically prior to the temporal sense (*in twenty minutes*; *in November*) and uses such as *in a difficult situation*, *fall in love*, and *take part in a competition*. It should be emphasized that all these uses are old, and date back to the earliest forms of English.

It is also possible to identify metaphors in the adverbial and prepositional particles of phrasal verbs (although they are often unanalysable). For example, phrasal verbs such as *melt away*, *wither away*, *fade out*, *fizzle out*, and *tail off* convey an idea of something disappearing or ending. The literal meanings of the particles relate to physical movement in a direction farther away from the speaker or an imagined base point, so that the metaphor here equates being at a distance or out of sight with coming to an end.

Chapter 3 looks further at metaphors of space and time, and Chapter 7 looks at the concept of grammatical metaphor.

METAPHOR, NEOLOGISMS, AND BORROWINGS

We have seen that many senses of words are metaphorical. In a similar way, new concepts or inventions may be named through the metaphorical usage of pre-existing words. A widely-discussed case, mentioned in Chapter 1, is that of computer terminology. In addition to *web*, *bug*, and *virus*, examples include *cookie*, *crash*, *firewall*, *icon*, *sprite*, *visit* (*a website*), *worm*, and many others: *phishing* is metaphorical, although the spelling has been changed. Another source of metaphorical neologisms is warfare. For example, the conflict in 2003 in Iraq contributed *rubber numbers* (imprecise or widely-varying figures of casualties, etc.) and *bug splat* (targeted bombing). *Mouseholing* has been used to refer to situations where troops are reluctant to enter buildings through doors or windows, in case of trip wires and booby traps, and so instead blow holes in the walls: any occupants are typically killed or maimed. Metaphor here is euphemistic: a sinister way of avoiding direct statement.

A related process is borrowing, where English adopts words and phrases from other languages. We have already discussed words such as *ecstasy*, *involve*, and *poppycock*, where, just as with *freelance* and *muddle*, the etymological roots show that a metaphorical process has happened; however, their metaphorical nature may not be obvious unless we examine their etymologies. Where English has borrowed metaphorical items from other languages, it has frequently borrowed only the metaphorical meanings, and not any literal meanings which may have existed in the source language. This can be shown most clearly with metaphorical borrowings which are marked out by their forms and often pronunciation as non-English. For example, *sangfroid* means 'composure, self-possession', and it comes from French, literally 'cold blood': compare the English expressions *in cold blood* and *cold-blooded* which refer to ruthlessness rather than composure. *In flagrante delicto* comes from Latin, literally 'in blazing crime', or 'in the heat of the crime': the English expressions *catch someone red-handed* or *a smoking gun* use different images but a related underlying metaphor. Metaphors in other languages will be discussed further in Chapter 6.

METAPHOR AND IDIOMS

Idioms are conventionalized phrases such as *spill the beans* or *jump the gun*, where the meaning of the whole phrase is different from the meaning which might be produced by interpreting the individual words in the phrase. These examples are metaphorical, and we will restrict our use of the term **idiom** to figurative phrases of this kind (*idiom* is sometimes used more generally to refer to any fixed phrase). Some idioms are more or less transparent, and we can see why they mean what they do; others are completely opaque, and their origins are obscure.

The following are typical of English idioms:

bury the hatchet

cost an arm and a leg

kick the bucket

make a mountain out of a molehill

on the cards

out of the blue

put the cart before the horse

rain cats and dogs

a red herring

twist someone round your little finger

In normal contexts, we are likely to interpret their idiomatic meanings without thinking about the metaphors that they contain. If we read or hear:

The monthly payments **cost an arm and a leg**.

(BoE)

we interpret it as an emphatic way of saying that the monthly payments are high. However, when we consider idioms from a metaphorical point of view, it is often possible to make sense of their idiomatic meanings, to appreciate how these meanings developed, and even to have mental images based on their metaphors.

This is easier in some cases than others. The metaphors in *cost an arm and a leg* and *twist someone round your little finger* are relatively transparent; in contrast, *kick the bucket* and *rain cats and dogs* are almost impossible to interpret. What has kicking buckets to do with death, and how can it rain cats and dogs, or how can heavy rain even resemble animals falling from the sky? (There are various theories about the origins of these peculiar expressions, but none has been proved satisfactorily.) It may still be possible to visualize even opaque idioms: for example, with *rain cats and dogs* we may have an image of cats and dogs falling like rain, perhaps reinforced by images seen in cartoons, advertisements, and so on, or the shower of frogs in the climactic sequences towards the end of the 1999 film *Magnolia*.

The wording of idioms is often fixed or frozen: for example, we do not find such variations as *rain dogs and cats*, *rain budgies and canaries*, *out of the green*, or *a yellow haddock*. (If we did, we would either try to interpret them literally, or assume that they were humorous, and re-interpret them in terms of the conventional idiom forms.) In other cases, there can be quite a lot of variation, and the idiom wording is unstable, although the metaphor and image remains the same. Corpus and text evidence shows up clusters of wordings such as the following:

the final/last nail in the coffin

to put another/a further nail in the coffin

hammer/drive/bang the last/first nail into someone's coffin (etc.)

nail down the coffin (lid)

one of the biggest nails in the coffin

wash your dirty linen in public

air your dirty laundry

do your dirty washing in public

launder your dirty washing

wash/air your linen/laundry in public

drag/hang out one's dirty laundry (etc.)

launder/air one's soiled/bloody linen (etc.)

As with other metaphors, if we interpret idioms literally, the meanings that we arrive at would be false, inappropriate, or impossible in the context. In fact, some could never be possible (*jump down someone's throat*, *move heaven and earth*), but use exaggeration or hyperbole to create their effect. There are a few idioms, however, which are always 'true'. To say that something is *not one's cup of tea* or that something is *not a bed of roses* is to be perfectly accurate. Nevertheless, the meanings of these idioms are still derived from the metaphors that they contain: what it might mean if something was indeed one's cup of tea or a bed of roses.

METAPHOR AND MEANING COMPONENTS

When we discussed topic, vehicle, and grounds in Chapter 1, we commented that only some prototypical features of the literal meanings are transferred in the metaphorical process, while others are suppressed: the example which we gave was *mountain*. These features are sometimes referred to as **meaning components**. If we consider the word *branch*, the transferred components relate to an idea of subsidiarity and connection – the idea that one thing is a subsidiary part of another, connected in some ways but also recognizably distinct. Components which are not transferred include botanical and real-world aspects of branches, such as the fact that they themselves subdivide into twigs, or have leaves, blossom, and fruit, or that birds sit on branches, and so on. If we consider the verb *to pigeonhole*, as in the following BoE examples:

> Maria was an artist, [. . .] but the work she did had nothing to do with creating objects commonly defined as art. Some people called her a photographer, others referred to her as a conceptualist, still others considered her a writer, but none of these descriptions was accurate, and in the end I don't think she can be **pigeonholed** in any way.

> if you ever tried to **pigeonhole** their sound, you'd come up with something like reggae/hardcore/funk/indie/reggae/metal/dance . . . and then you'd stop.

meaning components have been transferred from the original noun use, with reference to a structure with a series of compartments for pigeons to rest or nest in. The ideas of limited physical space and imposed, ordered, placement are transferred to the metaphorical verb, and recast in terms of limited scope or flexibility and imposed categorization.

However, any neutral or positive aspects of the original use, such as the practicality of housing pigeons in this way, are lost; instead, the metaphorical use takes on a negative quality, where categories are seen as restricting and even misleading.

Similarly with other words mentioned, such as *cream*, *fossil*, *float*, *hollow*, *juicy*, *magnetic*, or the idiom *make a mountain out of a molehill*: some components are transferred from literal to metaphorical meanings, and some are suppressed, while new components may be added. These new components may include evaluations, either positive or negative. For example, *hollow* in its core sense is simply descriptive of a physical structure, and is neutral in evaluative orientation; however, its metaphorical uses exploit the idea of emptiness and a lack of solidity or density as purely negative qualities:

> But the glossy choreography could not conceal a certain **hollow** centre to the performance.
>
> (BoE)

> Life will become increasingly **hollow** and pointless if you carry on like this.
>
> (BoE)

> He tried to sound confident, but he knew his assurances were **hollow**.
>
> (BoE)

We would use different words – and concepts – altogether if we wanted to express a positive idea of hollowness: perhaps *resonant* or *open*, or even *receptive* in some contexts. Similarly, the metaphorical sense of *cream* is entirely positive, and suppresses or hides any idea that the food cream is fatty, sickly, or unhealthy. Finally, evaluative orientations and the significance of transferred meaning components may well vary according to viewpoint: in the case of those metaphorical neologisms from warfare, *bug splat* and *mouseholing*, the troops, the targets, and we as readers are likely to have very different opinions.

METAPHOR AND FUZZY MEANINGS

We may have given the impression that metaphors have fixed or specific meanings, which can be contrasted with literal meanings, or neatly broken down into components. However, we suggested at the end of Chapter 1 that one of the things which makes metaphor so powerful as a communicative device is its imprecision or fuzziness. Whether we are using metaphor as writers/speakers, or whether we are interpreting it as readers/hearers, we manipulate metaphorical meanings with more latitude than we would literal meanings. This applies to conventional metaphors as well as creative ones: consider how much less precise *hollow* and *cream* are when metaphorical than when literal. This is, perhaps, because only some of the literal meaning's components are transferred in the metaphorical process, and these components often correspond to prototypical or idealized features of the literal. Imprecision seems to be the natural result.

Dan Sperber and Deirdre Wilson (1986) use the term **loose talk** to describe imprecision in language, and they argue that metaphor is simply one form of this. Although *loose talk* is itself a metaphorical and ambiguous phrase, it refers here not to indiscreet or woolly language, but to language which is flexible and versatile. Meanings are not fixed, but open to reinterpretation, depending on the context, and looseness becomes an important factor in relation to successful communication between speaker/writer and reader/hearer.

We can perhaps illustrate this most clearly with creative uses of figurative language. Compare, for example, our discussion of the 'silver bullet' metaphor in Chapter 1, or the following, taken from spoken interaction:

> The only thing was they give you a pittance. You know they didn't even give you enough for one day never mind anything else. So really it's sort of like erm you know it's like putting an arm to help you but just as you fell [*sic*] to grab it they draw it back.

(BoE)

The (male) speaker uses a simile to try to explain his viewpoint, and other items such as *you know* and *sort of* demonstrate his hesitancy and uncertainty as he does so. This is not actually a precise description, although the comparison might make it seem precise. 'Looseness' of language here is facilitating communication.

METAPHOR, EXPLOITATION, AND RELITERALIZATION

So far, we have been thinking explicitly about the metaphoricity of conventional metaphors: an unnatural exercise. However, there are times when even in ordinary usage we become aware of their metaphoricity, for example when someone makes a pun or tells a joke which exploits the literal/metaphorical ambiguity. For instance, an old joke about social class in Britain runs:

> Why is the aristocracy known as the cream of society?
> Because it's rich and thick and full of clots.

The entertainment value of Colemanballs (in the magazine *Private Eye*) lies in the way in which a speaker inadvertently mixes or confuses metaphors, or creates a clash between literal and metaphorical meanings:

> With regard to the broken finger, when batting I'll just have to play it by ear.
> Rooney's got the world at his feet, if he can keep his feet on the ground.
> He's not the sharpest sandwich in the picnic.
> Messner was a great mountaineer, but now he's 59. Surely he's past his peak?
> That sniper story . . . some bullet points . . .
> The people of Northern Ireland should step back and ask themselves have they moved on . . .
>
> (Fantoni (ed.) *Colemanballs 12*, 2004)

Conversely, we may realize that the word or phrase we are using will be interpreted metaphorically, rather than literally. The words *literal/literally* are sometimes used to indicate that we are not being metaphorical:

> In space, you can find methanol in **literally astronomical** quantities.
>
> (BoE)

> The country is now witnessing unprecedented trials of the military, and **literally truckloads** of secret documents are being released.
>
> (BoE)

Literally, however, is more often used simply to add emphasis to an exaggerated or hyperbolic statement, while acknowledging its metaphoricity:

> Everywhere public space is disappearing. Everywhere the city streets are becoming meaner and the city just **literally bristles with malice**.
>
> (BoE)

> One way or another our future is moving towards Europe. Technological change, plus increased communication and travel have **literally shrunk the world**.
>
> (BoE)

There are other formulae too which we use in similar ways: *proverbial* (which rarely co-occurs with proverbs), *so to speak*, *figurative/figuratively*, and, in speech, *if you like*. These also emphasize meaning, mark hesitation about a choice of wording, or indicate that we have said something ambiguous or made a pun.

> I have seen some cynical tactics in my time, but this **takes the proverbial biscuit**.
>
> (BoE)

> Unheard for 400 years, the Cornish bagpipes are now making a comeback, **getting a second wind so to speak**.
>
> (BoE)

> **Books have nourished me literally as well as figuratively** – I have made my living by editing other people's books since I graduated from college in 1965.
>
> (BoE)

> Because at the end of the day the most logical structure is the clinical directorate structure because that firmly puts the clinician ... **in the driving seat if you like**.
>
> (BoE)

Finally, conventional metaphorical expressions can be **reliteralized** in context, so that literal meaning is either reclaimed, or co-exists with the metaphorical one. For example, the following lines are taken from a poem 'The Field Hospital' by the Irish poet Paul Muldoon:

> We answer to no grey South
>
> Nor blue North, not self defence,
> The lie of just wars, neither
> Cold nor hot blood's difference
> In their discharging of guns ...
> > (Muldoon 1996: 14)

In cold blood, *cold-blooded*, and *hot-blooded* are conventional metaphors. However, the collocation *Cold nor hot blood's* and its contrasting of *cold* and *hot* makes us react to the underlying connection between literal and metaphorical meanings as if these are creative metaphors.

SUMMARY

In this chapter, we have looked at the ways in which metaphorical meaning is conventionalized in words and idioms. This can arise through simple processes of the development of multiple meanings and of the 'freezing' of metaphorical expressions, so that they recur with non-literal meanings and in fixed or semi-fixed formulations. More remotely in time, and often less obviously, metaphors can be traced back to the etymological roots of words. We do not analyse conventional metaphors in ordinary usage, and we are normally unconscious of their figurativeness; there are, however, times when writers/speakers become aware that they are using metaphorical items, and so indicate this in some way.

The very process of examining conventional metaphors often alerts us to hidden meanings, such as evaluative orientation or ideological position. In later chapters, we will consider how all this relates to creative metaphors too, and we will look further at the understanding and interpretation of metaphors (Chapter 5), and the implications of metaphor use in text (Chapters 7 and 8). First, in Chapter 3, we will look at how metaphors work systematically.

FURTHER READING

Aitchison, J. (2002) *Words in the Mind: an Introduction to the Mental Lexicon*, 3rd edn, Oxford: Blackwell. (Takes a psycholinguistic approach to word meaning: see, for example, Chapter 4, and Chapter 13, which deals with metaphor.)

Carter, R. (2004) *Language and Creativity: the Art of Common Talk*, London: Routledge. (Chapter 4 deals with 'figures of speech'.)

Chantrell, G. (ed.) (2002) *The Oxford Dictionary of Word Histories*, Oxford: Oxford University Press. (Very readable account of the historical origins and developments of 12,000 English words, listed in alphabetical order.)

Pyles, T. and Algeo, J. (1993) *The Origins and Development of the English Language*, 4th edn, Fort Worth, Texas: Harcourt Brace Jovanovich. (Chapters 10 and 12 deal with historical changes in word meaning and vocabulary.)

Sperber, D. and Wilson, D. (1986) 'Loose talk', *Proceedings of the Aristotelian Society* 86 (1985–6), 153–171. (For discussion of fuzzy meaning, and the continuum between literal and metaphorical.)

SYSTEMATIZING METAPHOR

In Chapter 1, we considered the example

> Scientists believe stress may suppress development of T-cells, the white blood cells which help to fight off invading micro-organisms.

and we commented on how our understanding of a biological process is made possible through a metaphor of warfare: the micro-organisms are conceptualized as adversaries and a body's response to them is conceptualized as a fight. In fact, this metaphorical conceptualization extends beyond this particular context. It is represented in conventional metaphors in the following BoE examples:

> died last week . . . after a long **battle** against cancer . . .

> **fell victim** to peritonitis aged just 36.

> the body has its own **defence** mechanism called the immune system to enable it to **fight off** untoward conditions.

> Deaths from malaria would almost double if the disease developed **resistance** to all available drugs.

> others say it helps to **combat** depression and side effects of the Pill.

and in the creative metaphors in this one:

> [The newly-isolated peptide] could be used as a **missile** to carry other **lethal warheads** to brain cancer cells ... It slides off the good cells, and therefore only kills the bad cells.
>
> (BoE)

We also talk about *heart attacks* and *bouts of illness*, *aggressive therapies* and *treatments*, and patients being *bombarded* with antibiotics. (See Montgomery 1991 for a discussion of the historical development of this metaphor.)

What we have here is evidence of a systematic transfer of lexical items from the semantic field of war to that of illness. There are two ways of interpreting this. We could simply say that many of the English words which refer to war and fighting are polysemous and happen to have developed secondary metaphorical senses to do with illness. But a more powerful way of looking at it is to say, as we have suggested, that in order to talk about illness we use the metaphors of war: that our understanding of illness is at least partly shaped by our understanding of war, and that we see an interaction between organisms – a biological process – as a fight, rather than any other kind of activity or process. So we can say that metaphor not only facilitates understanding but mediates it too. It is this second approach to metaphor, one particularly associated with the scholar George Lakoff, which we will explore in this chapter.

'METAPHORS WE LIVE BY': LAKOFF, JOHNSON, AND CONCEPTUAL METAPHOR

George Lakoff and Mark Johnson's book *Metaphors we Live by*, first published in 1980, is generally credited with establishing a new approach to the study of metaphor. (Lakoff and Johnson themselves acknowledge the work of Michael Reddy in stimulating their own work.) Since 1980, Lakoff has developed this approach in a series of publications, including collaborations with Mark Johnson, Mark Turner, and Zoltán Kövecses: many other scholars have also contributed to the exploration of metaphor along these lines. In this chapter, we will discuss the original book by Lakoff and Johnson, along with adjustments which they made in an afterword to the second edition (2003); we will also refer briefly to some other major contributions.

Lakoff and Johnson's starting point is that metaphor is an 'ordinary' part of language, not 'extraordinary'. They state that

> We have found [. . .] that metaphor is pervasive in everyday life, not just in language but in thought and action.
>
> (Lakoff and Johnson 1980/2003: 3)

and

> Our ordinary conceptual system, in terms of which we both think and act, is fundamentally metaphorical in nature.
>
> (1980/2003: 3)

Although many of their examples, and the examples which we will discuss, involve *language*, it is central to their argument that metaphor is a kind of *thinking* or conceptualization, not limited to language; however, language provides a convenient way to observe how metaphor works (see Chapter 9 for discussion of non-linguistic examples). As with the cases which we looked at in Chapter 2, we are normally unaware of the metaphoricity of our conceptual systems.

Their first example relates to a metaphorical conceptualization, or **conceptual metaphor**, ARGUMENT IS WAR. (Conceptual metaphors are conventionally written in capital letters, with the metaphorical concept mentioned first.) They use this to demonstrate how a concept can be metaphorical and structure an everyday activity. They give the following, often-quoted, examples of expressions in which ARGUMENT IS WAR appears:

> Your claims are *indefensible*.
>
> He *attacked every weak point* in my argument.
>
> His criticisms were *right on target*.
>
> I *demolished* his argument.
>
> I've never *won* an argument with him.
>
> You disagree? Okay, *shoot*!
>
> If you use that *strategy*, he'll *wipe you out*.
>
> He *shot down* all of my arguments.

They assert that these represent far more than metaphorical linguistic expressions: to quote them,

> Many of the things we *do* in arguing are partially structured by the concept of war.

(Lakoff and Johnson 1980/2003: 4)

That is, the way in which we conduct arguments is conditioned by the way in which we conduct wars. They suggest that if our culture conceptualized arguments through a different metaphor – maybe a dance – then the discourse structure of arguments would be different. An argument structured as a war consists of sequences of attacks and counter-attacks, with winning as the goal, but an argument structured like a dance might prioritize aesthetics and balance, and have different goals. In the 2003 edition of their book, they broaden the conceptualization into ARGUMENT IS STRUGGLE, but the underlying linkage between physical conflict and verbal conflict remains the same.

There are several important points to stress. First, these are *conceptual* metaphors, and they relate to concepts, not to individual lexical items. The metaphor ARGUMENT IS WAR (or STRUGGLE) links the conceptualization of 'argument' to that of 'war' or 'struggle'. The fact that the metaphorical expression *a war of words* means 'argument' is almost irrelevant. While it provides linguistic evidence of the conceptual metaphor, the metaphorical link is between the underlying concept areas WAR and ARGUMENT, not the individual items *war of words* and *argument*.

Second, the conceptual metaphor ARGUMENT IS WAR/STRUGGLE is simply one example, and there are many more relating to further aspects of human life: conversation in general, truth and morality, knowledge and education, and so on. More significantly, many conceptual metaphors relate to abstract phenomena which are difficult to define or describe. Just as a metaphor of war enables us to conceptualize illness, other metaphors enable us to conceptualize life experiences, emotions, qualities, problems, and thought itself. Metaphor therefore seems to be a normal part of the conceptualization process: as Lakoff and Johnson put it, 'Our ordinary conceptual system [. . .] is fundamentally metaphorical in nature'.

Third, conceptual metaphors may be culture-specific. Saying that *we* view argument as war or illness as an adversary is to say that Anglophone Western society does. Other cultures may view argument and illness quite differently. At the same time, some metaphors seem to be universal, and this is strong support for Lakoff and Johnson's claim about human conceptual systems. We will come back to this point later on in this chapter, and we will deal further with crosscultural and cross-linguistic issues in Chapter 6.

ANALYSING CONCEPTUAL METAPHORS

In Chapter 1, we introduced the traditional terms *topic*, *vehicle*, and *grounds* for elements in a metaphor: respectively, the meaning, the linguistic expression, and the similarities or connections between them. However, a different set of terms is used to identify the elements involved in conceptual metaphors, and these reflect the very different theoretical approach.

Conceptual metaphors equate two concept areas, as in ARGUMENT IS WAR. The term **source domain** is used for the concept area from which the metaphor is drawn: here, WAR. **Target domain** is used for the concept area to which the metaphor is applied: here, ARGUMENT. (Compare the use of the terms **source** and **target** with respect to translation, where the language of the original text is regarded as source, and the language into which it is translated as target: we can compare the process of translation with the process of re-structuring or re-stating one concept in terms of another.)

Conceptual metaphor theory sees the connections between concept areas in terms of **correspondences** or **mappings** between elements within source and target domains. For example, a typical feature in the concept area or source domain WAR is a defensive barricade or line of soldiers (concepts here represent 'idealized', traditional, notions of war). In the target domain ARGUMENT, this corresponds to or maps onto the data, facts, or beliefs which someone has and uses to sub-stantiate their position. Similarly, barricades and lines of soldiers have weak points, which adversaries try to find and attack in order to win: these map onto weak points in arguments – incomplete data, incorrect information, or false beliefs. Hence we can talk about *lines of defence* and *outflanking* or *outmanoeuvring* adversaries in both warfare and argu-ment. Not all aspects of a source necessarily map onto the target: some mappings are much more extensive than others.

It is easy to think of correspondences and mappings in terms of similarities between elements in domains. However, Lakoff and Johnson believe that conceptual metaphors are not based on similarities, but on the correlating elements in source and target domains: if there seem to be similarities, they derive from those correlations, not the other way around. The use of the terms *correspondence* or *mapping*, then, helps ensure that in analysing conceptual metaphors, connections are made between aspects, features, or roles in source and target domains at a *conceptual* level. Note that other theories of metaphor have different views of 'similarity', and the relationship between simile and metaphor, as we will see in Chapter 5.

METAPHORS AND TIME

The second case which Lakoff and Johnson discuss is TIME IS MONEY (or TIME IS A RESOURCE/COMMODITY). The phenomenon time is difficult to explain non-scientifically; however, we conceptualize it metaphorically as a physical commodity and something which we can possess, use, acquire, or lose. Lakoff and Johnson give the following examples:

> You're *wasting* my time.
>
> I don't *have* the time to *give* you.
>
> How do you *spend* your time these days?
>
> That flat tire *cost* me an hour.
>
> I've *invested* a lot of time in her.
>
> I don't *have enough* time to *spare* for that.
>
> You're *running out* of time.
>
> You need to *budget* your time.

These are common, unremarkable, uses of words: some such as *have, give*, and *enough* barely seem metaphorical at all.

This is not the only way in which we conceptualize time, and some other traditional metaphorical expressions to do with time include:

> Time is a great healer.
>
> It's a race against time.
>
> The sands of time are running out.

Had any of these conceptualizations developed as extensively as TIME IS MONEY, we might conceive of time quite differently. How might the mappings of TIME IS A DOCTOR or TIME IS A COMPETITOR have worked? *The sands of time* refers to traditional hour-glasses: but would it be possible for a basic conception of time to be in terms of grains of sand, something which forms through a process of fragmentation and is unstable, heaped up or levelled out by natural forces, capable of swallowing things up or of being shaped into walls or sandcastles, ultimately collapsing or being blown or washed away? However difficult it is to think about, we need to remember that TIME IS MONEY represents just one conceptualization of time. It happens that in English what we do with time is to *pass* or *spend* it: these are its commonest verb collocates. In French, the literal equivalent of *spend* is *dépenser* but it is not used about time: French speakers would use the verb *passer* 'pass' or, in translating a context such as 'spend time doing something', the verb *consacrer*, which is cognate with the English verb *consecrate* and could be back-translated as 'devote (time to something)'.

In fact, the collocation of *pass* and *time* represents another conceptual metaphor, one which in this case does seem to be universal rather than language- or culture-specific. Time is generally conceptualized as if it had physical dimensions or is physically located in space: the ways in which we talk about time are similar to the ways in which we talk about distance and position. In addition to *passing time*, or *time passing*, there are verb uses such as *years go by*, *Christmas is coming*, *the end of term is approaching*, *the holidays came and went*, *how do you fill your time?*; noun uses such as *at this point in time*, *over the course of time*, *a length of time*, *a time span*; and adjectival uses such as *long*, *lengthy*, *short*, *drawn-out*. Their metaphoricity is relatively obvious once we begin to think about it. We pointed out in Chapter 2 that grammatical words may also have metaphorical meanings: many prepositions and adverbs have literal meanings which are spatial, and metaphorical meanings relating to time. Examples here include *in the weeks ahead*, *in April*, *at the weekend*, *on Sunday*, *within eight months*, *quarter past nine* (compare American English *quarter before nine* and *quarter after nine*), *looking back* into the past, or *looking ahead/forward* to the future, and *five years ago* (etymologically linked to the verb *go*).

METAPHORS OF COMMUNICATION AND UNDERSTANDING

We said earlier that the work of Michael Reddy contributed to the development of this approach to metaphor: in particular, a paper first published in 1979. In this paper, Reddy drew attention to the metaphorical way in which we talk about communication, and the effect which this has on our thinking. He writes:

> [The] evidence suggests that English has a preferred framework for conceptualizing communication, and can bias thought process toward this framework, even though nothing more than common sense is necessary to devise a different, more accurate framework.
>
> (Reddy 1993: 165)

Reddy refers to this framework as the **conduit metaphor**, and analyses its major features as follows:

(1) language functions like a conduit . . . ;
(2) in writing and speaking, people insert their thoughts or feelings in the words;
(3) words accomplish the transfer by containing the thoughts or feelings and conveying them to others; and
(4) in listening or reading, people extract the thoughts and feelings once again from the words.

> (Reddy 1993: 170)

That is, we conceptualize communication as a *transfer* of thoughts, words, and ideas from one person to another and as if those thoughts, ideas, and words have physical substance – in the way that a substance might be transferred from one place to another along a conduit. He says that, based on his evidence, 70 per cent of English words and phrases to do with communication are instances of the conduit metaphor. Amongst Reddy's examples are:

> Try to *get* your *thoughts across* better.
>
> Try to *pack* more *thoughts into* fewer *words.*
>
> The *sentence was filled with emotion.*
>
> Let me know if you *find* any good *ideas in* the *essay.*

In his paper, Reddy goes on to discuss the social and cultural implications of the conduit metaphor, including ways in which the conduit metaphor is harmful rather than helpful, especially in relation to developments in mass communication. For example, the metaphor encourages us to think that the more information we transfer or store, the more successfully we are communicating; yet in fact, successful communication depends on whether the receiver understands, not how much they have received. In an extended discussion, he argues that we think of our cultural heritage in terms of books and so on, containing knowledge and ideas, with libraries representing 'repositories' of culture, but this is a misleading view of culture. To paraphrase his discussion, it is not enough to have knowledge stored in a library; we also need people who are able to understand, interpret, and use it. His observation has other parallels now, in the internet era. Search engines make it easy to retrieve enormous quantities of information through electronic 'conduits'; however, information alone is not enough, and we need techniques, tools, and considerable analytical skills in order to make use of the information and so for the communication of information to succeed.

The conduit metaphor is a basic metaphor of communication: several aspects of it can be explored through further conceptual metaphors relating to knowledge and understanding. For example, just as we conceptualize communication as 'containing' data, we think of our minds as containers and having spatial dimensions. Thoughts *enter our heads* or *cross our minds*; we talk about *cramming* for examinations, or *filling our heads with facts*; and we *search our memories* or have vague recollections *in the back of our minds*. Similarly, we conceptualize the process of understanding in terms of sight or touch, as if what we understand has some kind of physical reality. The metaphors can be stated as UNDERSTANDING IS SEEING or UNDERSTANDING IS HOLDING, and some of the many conventional lexical realizations in English are:

see what someone means, see someone's point

look at the facts

recognize that there is a problem

insight, foresight, perception

getting to grips with a problem

a grasp of a subject

put one's finger on something

kick an idea around

The same metaphors can be traced in the etymologies of further words which refer to understanding, such as *clarify*, *elucidate*, *illuminate*; and *comprehend*, *(in)tangible*.

METAPHORS AND EMOTIONS

Our final examples of conceptual metaphors relate to the conceptualization of emotion. Just as with thoughts, words, and ideas, we think of emotions as if they have physical substance or presence: we *have* feelings, or *are filled with* emotion, love, pride, rage, we react to things *with* astonishment, anger, enthusiasm, we fall *in* love. When something affects us emotionally, we conceptualize it as if it has a physical impact on us: news *hits* us hard, we are *struck* or *touched* by events, actions, and people, or *bowled over* or *knocked out* by them (compare our comments on literal and metaphorical senses of *impress/impression* in Chapter 2). Lakoff and Johnson express this as EMOTIONAL EFFECT IS PHYSICAL CONTACT (1980/2003: 50).

Individual emotions are also conceptualized metaphorically. For example, affection and love are conceptualized in terms of heat and fire, and relationships in general in terms of physical proximity and connections. There are many expressions, conventional metaphors, which demonstrate this:

a warm welcome

she was very cool/cold/frosty with us

a red-hot lover

be on heat

inflame someone's passions

smoulder with desire

a close relationship

inseparable friends

a rift between them

they broke up

Anger, too, is conceptualized in terms of HEAT, including notions of redness and of heated fluid or steam in a container:

a heated argument

a fiery temper

flare up

hot under the collar

see red

scarlet with annoyance

blow one's top

explode

make someone's blood boil

Happiness and sadness are conceptualized in terms of UP/DOWN (or HIGH/LOW) and LIGHT/DARK:

on a high

raise someone's spirits

things are looking up

feel low

downcast

depressed

shining eyes

future is bright

dark thoughts

a sombre mood

Extended discussion of these and other metaphorical conceptualizations of emotions can be found in Kövecses (2000; also 2002: 85ff. and elsewhere), and Lakoff (1987: 380ff.).

TYPES OF CONCEPTUAL METAPHOR

In the 1980 edition of *Metaphors we Live by*, Lakoff and Johnson identify three categories of conceptual metaphors: **structural**, **orientational**, and **ontological**. Because these terms and categories are used in the literature on metaphor, we will discuss them briefly, before considering how Lakoff and Johnson revised them later.

ARGUMENT IS WAR is an example of a **structural metaphor**. According to Lakoff and Johnson, structural metaphors are 'cases where one concept is metaphorically structured in terms of another' (1980/ 2003: 14). Source domains supply frameworks for target domains: these determine the ways in which we think and talk about the entities and activities to which the target domains refer, and even the ways in which we behave or carry out activities, as in the case of argument.

An **orientational metaphor**, according to Lakoff and Johnson, 'organizes a whole system of concepts with respect to one another' (1980/2003: 14). It typically involves an orientational or spatial concept of some kind, such as up/down and in/out. Two examples are HAPPY IS UP/SAD IS DOWN, which we have just considered, and MORE IS UP/LESS IS DOWN. In each case, the target concepts are paired just as the source concepts are: they are antonyms or counterparts. Lakoff and Johnson give these examples for MORE IS UP/LESS IS DOWN:

> The number of books printed each year keeps going *up*.
>
> My income *rose* last year.
>
> The number of errors he made is incredibly *low*.
>
> If you're too hot, turn the heat *down*.

UP/DOWN orientational metaphors recur in a number of other target domains: CONSCIOUS IS UP, HEALTH AND LIFE ARE UP, HAVING CON-TROL OR FORCE IS UP, HIGH STATUS IS UP, GOOD IS UP, and their opposites. Lakoff and Johnson claim – and research generally supports this – that many of these metaphors are universal rather than culture-specific.

Ontological metaphors allow us to conceptualize and talk about things, experiences, and processes, however vague or abstract they are, as if they have definite physical properties. Lakoff and Johnson say:

> Once we can identify our experiences as entities or substances, we can refer to them, categorize them, group them, and quantify them – and by this means, reason about them.
>
> (Lakoff and Johnson 1980/2003: 25)

Metaphorical conceptualizations of time, communication, and under-standing are cases in point. This is similar to the conceptualization of abstract qualities as if they were objects: we *have*, *acquire*, or *lose* qualities and attributes such as beauty, wisdom, or a reputation. Finally, we conceptualize something that is difficult and problematic as if it has physical form or else an illness: for example, we talk about *facing problems*, *ironing out difficulties*, *teasing out tricky areas*; *a remedy for a problem*, *a sick society*, *a headache for the government*.

There are overlaps between these three categories. Structural metaphors and orientational metaphors may have ontological functions too, while ontological metaphors depend on having structured source domains. In fact, in the afterword to the second edition of their book, Lakoff and Johnson refer to their earlier categorization as 'artificial', arguing that all conceptual metaphors are structural and ontological: they also comment that many conceptual metaphors are orientational (see Lakoff and Johnson 2003. 264–265).

SYSTEMATICITY

The idea that metaphors are systematic is fundamental to conceptual metaphor theory. But the sheer numbers of different metaphors, of which we have considered just a few, sometimes give the impression of a lack of system. This impression may be particularly strong in cases of multiple mappings, when a single source domain provides conceptualizations for multiple target domains (WAR for both ARGUMENT and ILLNESS) or a single target domain is conceptualized by multiple source domains (TIME as both COMMODITY and SPACE). There are cases, too, of many-to-many mappings (HAPPY IS UP, HAPPY IS LIGHT; MORE IS UP, UNDERSTANDING IS LIGHT), and of domains being both sources and targets (ILLNESS IS WAR, PROBLEMS ARE ILLNESSES). One challenge for conceptual metaphor theory is to show that such metaphors are consistent or coherent, not contradictory, and in the next section, we will discuss how multiple mappings can be compatible with one another. First we will look at how creative, conventional, and idiosyncratic metaphors fit into systems, and then at different levels of generality in conceptual metaphors.

Most of the linguistic examples which Lakoff and Johnson use, or which we have given, are conventional metaphors: institutionalized senses of polysemous words (*attack*, *see*, *spend*), fixed phrases of different kinds (*shoot down*, *put one's finger on*, *hot under the collar*), and a few etymological metaphors (*elucidate*, *intangible*). While this is a convenient way to demonstrate systematicity, creative non-institutionalized metaphors may also be systematic. The following BoE examples include both conventional and creative metaphors (the metaphor in the second one is partly expressed through simile), and relate to aspects of the conceptual metaphors ARGUMENT IS WAR, TIME IS SPACE, and ANGER IS HEAT:

> And so Max flagellated us with the purist's cudgel, but just as often, I suspect, he wielded it stringently at himself.

> a future stretching out as broad and as bright as a beach at sunrise.

> My anger flared again ... Something stirred in the seething stew of my thoughts.

A further example is a widely-discussed conceptual metaphor which we have not yet mentioned: LIFE IS A JOURNEY. Conventional metaphors for birth, death, and experiences in between include ideas of travelling and movement: babies *arrive*, or are said to be *on the way*; the dead are referred to as *the departed* or are said to have *gone*; we talk about *moving on* and *getting ahead* in our lives, about having *direction* and *reaching* particular ages or *milestones*, about rites of *passage* and the *courses* of our lives. Creative metaphors here can be found not just in single phrases or sentences but as whole texts, framed round a journey which is used to represent or symbolize life in some way. Language-based examples range from songs (The Beatles' *Long and Winding Road*, Lynyrd Skynyrd's *Freebird*, Joni Mitchell's *Woodstock*) to books and plays (Cervantes' *Don Quixote*, Tolkien's *Lord of the Rings*, Beckett's *Waiting for Godot*). We will look at some non-verbal examples in Chapter 9.

However, not all metaphors fit neatly into systematic sets, and some are idiosyncratic. Perhaps the most useful approach to these is to analyse them in terms of very general modes of conceptualization, rather than over-specific ones. For example, we could say that the idiom *put the cart before the horse* represents a conceptual metaphor DOING SOMETHING IN THE WRONG ORDER IS HARNESSING AN ANIMAL INCORRECTLY, but a better analysis would be in terms of temporal sequences corresponding to physical positions, and relating to TIME IS SPACE. And when a critic reviewing a novel says that themes

> are tossed into [John] Irving's literary wok, then spiced with the paprika of his
> black humour and stirfried in his extraordinary imagination.
>
> (BoE)

it is possible to identify a specific conceptual metaphor INTELLECTUAL
QUALITIES ARE SPICES, a broader metaphor WRITING IS COOKING, and
a very general one where creative, verbal, and intellectual processes
are conceptualized metaphorically as physical ones.

Systematizing metaphors in this way, in fact, helps clarify the
consistent patterns in metaphorical conceptualization. For example,
both ARGUMENT IS WAR and the conduit metaphor relate to a more
general VERBAL IS PHYSICAL metaphor. Orientational metaphors with
UP/DOWN have extensive sets of mappings for individual target
domains, and a more general tendency is for UP metaphors to be positive (MORE/HAPPINESS/CONSCIOUSNESS/POWER IS UP) and counterparts with DOWN to be negative (LESS/SADNESS/UNCONSCIOUSNESS/
POWERLESSNESS IS DOWN): see further in Chapter 7. These very general
conceptualizations are some of the most interesting of all, particularly
in terms of what they reveal about basic processes of human thought.

HIGHLIGHTING AND HIDING

When we looked at word meaning in Chapter 2, we said that generally
only some meaning components are transferred from literal meanings
to metaphorical ones. Conceptual metaphor theory uses the term
highlighting to refer to the selective mapping of source domain
features onto target domains: the suppression of other features is
termed **hiding** (see Lakoff and Johnson 1980/2003: 10ff.). The concept areas of source and target domains are complex, and different
aspects are highlighted in different metaphors. So when a source or
target domain has multiple mappings, the individual mappings represent different sets of highlighted features. For example, Lakoff and
Johnson point out that the UP/DOWN source domain relates to many
different target domains, but these target domains highlight and exploit
different kinds of 'up-ness'.

Lakoff and Johnson discuss highlighting and multiple mapping in
relation to ARGUMENT, and four source domains (1980/2003: 87ff.).
In addition to the domain WAR, they consider the metaphors AN

ARGUMENT IS A JOURNEY, AN ARGUMENT IS A CONTAINER, and AN ARGUMENT IS A BUILDING: these relate to logical or academic argument, rather than quarrels. The metaphors are not in conflict with each other, but each foregrounds different correspondences between sources and targets. Just as ARGUMENT IS WAR highlights conflict and the business of winning or losing, AN ARGUMENT IS A JOURNEY highlights the goal (or destination) of an argument, and the process by which the goal is achieved or reached; AN ARGUMENT IS A CONTAINER highlights the content of the argument, and its shape or form; and AN ARGUMENT IS A BUILDING highlights the strength and structure of an argument. Their examples include

> We will *proceed* in a *step-by-step* fashion.
>
> *So far*, we have seen that no current theories will work.
>
> You don't have *much of* an argument, but his objections have even *less substance*.
>
> Your argument *won't hold water*.
>
> You've got the *framework* for a *solid* argument.
>
> He is trying to *buttress* his argument with a lot of irrelevant facts . . .

See Lakoff and Johnson (1980/2003: 87ff.); further in-depth discussion of these and other multiple mappings can be found in Kövecses (2002: 79ff.).

THE EXPERIENTIAL BASIS OF CONCEPTUAL METAPHORS

So far we have looked mainly at how conceptual metaphors work, rather than why specific metaphors should have developed in the first place. Theorists suggest that many conceptual metaphors can be related to very basic human experiences: what has been referred to as an **experiential** basis for metaphors. For example, an explanation for the metaphor ANGER IS HEAT can be found in the physical sensations produced by anger – rising temperature, altered breathing patterns, and so on. There also seem to be physical explanations for the orientational metaphors UP and DOWN. We are vertical when we are active and awake, but we lie down when we are ill, asleep, or unconscious (CONSCIOUS IS UP, SICK/UNCONSCIOUS IS DOWN); we stand straighter or move more 'floatingly' when we are happy, but slump or look down when we are unhappy (HAPPY IS UP, SAD IS DOWN); one person wins a fight by being physically on top of another and holding them down (POWERFUL IS UP, POWERLESS IS DOWN). MORE IS UP/LESS IS DOWN relates to the way in which greater quantities of things form larger, higher heaps. Lakoff explains KNOWING/UNDERSTANDING IS SEEING as 'most of what we know comes through vision, and in the overwhelming majority of cases, if we see something, then we know it is true' (1993: 240). See Lakoff and Johnson (1980/2003; 1999), and Kövecses (2002: 67ff. and elsewhere) for further discussion. The idea of such a basis for metaphor is important, and we will consider further aspects in Chapter 5.

SUMMARY

This chapter has provided a brief introduction to conceptual metaphor and the ideas of Lakoff and his colleagues. Amongst the key points are that metaphor operates concept-to-concept; it is systematic; it provides structures for our conceptual system and affects the ways in which we think about things; and it may have an experiential basis. Conceptual metaphor is not limited to language, although language can be used to demonstrate how it works. There are important implications relating to ideology (how we view the world) and to philosophy (the nature of thought itself).

The work of Lakoff and colleagues has been hugely influential, and we will discuss other aspects in later chapters. It is important to note, however, that the cognitive approach to metaphor has been criticized. Amongst the objections are that it is insufficiently rigorous; its analyses of conceptual metaphors often seem ad hoc; it pays insufficient attention to authentic data, including linguistic data; and its claims about thought are often unverified or unverifiable.

We have tried to show the strengths and range of conceptual metaphor theory. More than any other theory, it has integrated metaphor into mainstream semantics and linguistics, and shown how far-reaching it is. The enormous interest in figurative language at the present time can be directly attributed to Lakoff and colleagues, and their work. Perhaps an appropriate way to end this chapter is to list some of the many metaphors which we have used ourselves in writing it, in order to draw attention to what we were conceptualizing, how we were doing so, and what the significance is for the meaning of the text. For example, in this section alone, we have

> metaphor *operates*
>
> how we *view* the world
>
> the cognitive *approach*
>
> *mainstream* semantics and linguistics
>
> *shown* how *far-reaching* it is
>
> *enormous* interest *in* figurative language
>
> *at* the *present* time

and more.

FURTHER READING

Gibbs, R.W. (1994) *The Poetics of Mind: Figurative Thought, Language, and Understanding*, Cambridge: Cambridge University Press.

Gibbs, R.W. and Steen, G. (eds) (1999) *Metaphor in Cognitive Linguistics*, Amsterdam: John Benjamins.

Kövecses, Z. (2000) *Metaphor and Emotion: Language, Culture and Body in Human Feeling*, Cambridge: Cambridge University Press.

—— (2002) *Metaphor: a Practical Introduction*, Oxford: Oxford University Press.

Lakoff, G. (1993) 'The contemporary theory of metaphor', in A. Ortony (ed.) *Metaphor and Thought*, 2nd edn, Cambridge: Cambridge University Press: 202–251.

Lakoff, G. and Johnson, M. (1980; new edn 2003) *Metaphors we Live by*, Chicago: University of Chicago Press.

—— (1999) *Philosophy in the Flesh: the Embodied Mind and its Challenge to Western Thought*, New York: Basic Books. (Especially parts I and II.)

Reddy, M.J. (1993) 'The conduit metaphor: a case of frame conflict in our language about language', in A. Ortony (ed.) *Metaphor and Thought*, 2nd edn, Cambridge: Cambridge University Press: 164–201.

4

METONYMY

In Chapter 1, we introduced **metonymy** as a specific kind of figurative language. We explained it as involving either part-and-whole relations, such as using *hands* to refer to workers, or else naming by association, such as using *the stage* to refer to the theatrical profession. Metonymy is important in relation to the study of metaphor, and we will examine it in more detail in this chapter.

Here are some further examples of metonyms:

Metonym	Meaning
the Crown	the monarchy
plastic	credit cards
threads	clothes
wheels	vehicle
dish	form of prepared food
bricks and mortar	a house or other building
a roof over one's head	place to live

Wheels and *a roof over one's head* are like *hands*: the whole is referred to in terms of one of its constituent parts. In the cases of *threads*, and *bricks and mortar*, the whole is referred to in terms of the material that it is made out of. *Crown* is like *stage*, and names by association: it refers to an institution, rather than an individual king or queen, and denotes something symbolic that is associated with kings or queens, rather than an actual ceremonial headdress.

METONYMY AND SYNECDOCHE

We have used **metonymy** as a general term to refer to this kind of figurative language. However, **synecdoche** (pronounced /sin-**neck**-doe-key/) is sometimes used as a traditional term for part-and-whole metonymy. That is, synecdoche covers cases where the whole entity is referred to by the name of one of its constituent parts, or where a constituent part is referred to by the name of the whole. *Hands* is an example of the first of these; *Scotland have a great chance of winning the game*, where *Scotland* refers to a Scottish national sports team, is an example of the second.

Where the term *synecdoche* is used, *metonymy* has a narrower meaning, and refers just to the process of naming by association. So while *hands* = *workers* is an example of synecdoche, *stage* = *theatrical profession* and *Crown* = *the monarchy* would be examples of metonymy. However, it is often difficult to distinguish between metonymy and synecdoche. *Plastic* = *credit card* is a case of synecdoche because credit cards are made from plastic, but it is also metonymic because we use *plastic* to refer to the whole system of paying by means of a prearranged credit facility, not just the cards themselves. In fact, many scholars do not use synecdoche as a category or term at all. We will not use it in this book, but will continue to refer to both kinds of naming phenomenon – part-and-whole and naming-by-association – as metonymy.

METONYMY, POLYSEMY, AND MEANINGS

In Chapter 2, we saw that figurative processes often account for cases of polysemy. Just as many senses of polysemous words are metaphorical, many others are metonymic. The metonymic meanings of *hands*, *plastic*, *threads*, and *wheels* discussed above are subsidiary senses of *hand*, *plastic*, *thread*, and *wheel*, and not the core ones we would think of first.

There are some consistent patterns of metonymic transfer. A common one is where words which refer, very broadly, to some kind of container are also used to refer to the contents. At its simplest, *glass*, *jug*, *tin*, *packet*, and so on are frequently used to refer to what is in the glass, jug, tin, or packet: *drink three glasses a day, you'll probably need three tins to finish the job.* Words referring to buildings – *house, university, school, office, church* – can be used to refer to the people in the building, or to the institution or organization associated with the building: *the college was outraged by the news.* Similarly, the names of nations and peoples can be used to refer to their sports teams, armed forces, or other representatives: *Sweden 1, Argentina 1*; *Rome conquered Britain.* Words referring to forms of spoken or written matter, recorded music, art, and so on – *conversation, book, newspaper, letter, CD, painting* – can be used to refer to the intellectual or artistic content of what is spoken, written, recorded, or painted: *a fascinating book* as opposed to *a large book.* These kinds of metonymic transfer are almost grammatical in their regularity.

Other recurrent patterns in metonymic senses can be found with *hands, crown, stage*, where parts of the body represent the whole body or person, items of clothing represent a person or subgroup of people (regardless of what they are actually wearing), or aspects of work represent the workers. For example, we also talk of *head* of cattle, or counting *heads*; we use *eye(s)* to represent people paying attention, as in *all eyes were on her*; we use *blonde, brunette, redhead* to represent someone with hair of a particular colour; and some terms of insult are metonyms based on words for sexual organs and other parts of the body. In colloquial language, *suits* can refer to people, usually men, in power or in management, *skirt* to a young woman, considered in terms of her sexual attractiveness, and *anorak* to someone who is socially awkward and obsessional. Similarly, the *cloth* represents the clergy, especially of the Anglican Church; the *Bar* represents barristers in Britain (or the legal profession generally in the United States); and *sparks* and *chips* are colloquial terms for electricians and carpenters. There are parallel uses in expressions such as *blue collar* and *white collar* to refer respectively to manual/industrial and clerical/professional work, *chalkface* to refer to teaching, and *grease monkeys* to refer to mechanics (*monkey* here is metaphorical).

In most of the examples so far, the literal or core sense is fairly concrete, physical, or specific, while metonymic uses vary between concrete, abstract, and general. The following examples are of words referring to sounds, with metonymic uses referring to actual physical things: most of these are echoic, or developed through onomatopoeia, and the core or original sense is often a verb. *Fizz* and *pop* both refer metonymically to effervescent drinks, and *bubble-and-squeak*, a dish made by frying cooked potato and cabbage, refers to the noises made during the cooking process (compare metonymic uses of *bubbles* and *bubbly* to refer to champagne). Finally, *rattle* 'child's toy, instrument' developed from a verb referring to the noise it makes; and *patter* in expressions such as *the patter of tiny feet*, to refer to a planned or expected baby, is also metonymic.

METONYMY AND ETYMOLOGY

The historical development of metonymic senses of polysemous words is often fairly clear. As with metaphors, the original sense is typically the most concrete, physical sense, and may well still be the core or commonest sense. This is the case with many of the words we have mentioned so far, such as *crown*, *dish*, *hand*, *thread*, and *wheel*.

However, other cases are more complex. For most people, the dominant or core sense of the noun *train* is now a kind of vehicle: a locomotive and carriages or wagons which run on railway lines. The word *train* has a long, complicated history: its earliest sense, now obsolete, meant 'delay' or 'tarrying'. It also had early senses relating to dragging (it ultimately derives from a Latin verb *trahere* 'to drag'); to groups of people that follow behind someone or something, as in *a train of followers*; and to series of things that are dragged behind something or are strung together, as in *a wagon train*. After the invention of the railway, it was natural to talk about *a train of carriages* behind the locomotive, and this later became shortened to *train* and eventually to include the locomotive itself: a whole-for-part metonym (referring to a locomotive as an *engine* is also metonymic).

Like metaphors, metonyms may be concealed within etymologies. *Capitation* is an allowance paid to a school, health centre, and so on to provide services for a specified number of people: it derives from the Latin noun *caput* 'head' – as in the expression *per capita* – and metonymically refers to people in terms of their heads. *Map* derives from *mappa mundi*, literally 'sheet of the world', or the sheet, cloth, or parchment on which the world was drawn: it is a metonym in the same way that *plastic* and *threads* are. Words such as *surgeon* and *surgery* ultimately derive from Greek roots *kheir-* and *ergon*, respectively 'hand' and 'work': this is a very similar metonym to that involved in *hand* in the sense 'worker'.

The next example is especially complicated. *Cattle* refers to livestock: now only bovine livestock, although in Middle English it could also denote horses, sheep, and pigs – generally creatures regarded as property. This sense of *cattle* is connected with an earlier sense 'property, wealth', and is metonymic: the livestock are representative of the property or wealth. (Exactly the same metonym had existed in Old English, where *feoh* denoted both cattle and money or property.) Although the earlier 'property' sense no longer exists for *cattle*, it is still found in *chattels*, which historically is a variant of *cattle*, with a common origin in French. This in turn derives ultimately from Latin *capitalis, caput* 'relating to the head, head'. Both Latin *capitale* and modern English *capital* have a sense 'property, assets', which can be traced back to an idea of 'main' or 'most important' asset or source of wealth: thus a metaphorical sense led eventually to the development of later metonymic ones.

Finally, a few metonymic expressions from other languages have been adopted into English without changes in form. *Per capita* is one example; another is French *tête à tête* 'conversation', literally 'head to head'. *Head-to-head* itself is lexicalized in English, and also refers to a conversation: it has other meanings, too, to do with competition and opposition. However, *tête à tête* has connotations of intimacy or secrecy, where *head-to-head* has connotations of confrontation or negotiation.

METONYMS AND IDIOMS

In Chapter 2, we looked at idioms and proverbs which are metaphorical: they can be metonymic too, and *a roof over one's head* is a case in point. Many metonymic idioms and proverbs involve parts of the body: *hate someone's guts*, *two heads are better than one*, and *show one's face somewhere*. Items which mention a particular part of the body often share connotations or aspects of their meanings. For example, the word *heart* typically occurs in expressions to do with emotions and feelings, as in *absence makes the heart grow fonder*, *set one's heart on something*, and *lose one's heart to someone*. Others involve items of clothing or equipment. The idiom *hang up one's boots* typically refers to the retirement of a football player, and there are many possible variants, where *boots* is replaced by another item appropriate to the retiree: *gloves* (boxer), *microphone* (broadcaster), *helmet* (cyclist), *racquet* (tennis player), and so on.

This last idiom, like many of the others listed, is also metaphorical: the 'hanging up' is not literal, and *hang up one's boots* may be said of retirees other than sports players. In fact, there is often a complicated relationship between metonymy and metaphor, especially with those which mention parts of the body. *To fight tooth and nail for something* is metaphorical: no actual physical fight takes place, just some kind of intense activity towards a particular desired goal, and there may not be an actual human rival or enemy. We could express this metaphor in conceptual terms as INTENSE EFFORT IS WAR (compare the words *strive* and *strife*, which have a common etymology). At the same time, *to fight tooth and nail* is metonymic: two body parts are named, and stand for the whole person, or his or her actions. This can be illustrated further with a pair of idioms which may seem contradictory. If you say that people *get their hands dirty*, you mean that they get involved fully in some activity; if you say that people have *dirty* (or *bloody*) *hands*, you mean that they are guilty of something. The first of these implies admiration, the second, condemnation. The idioms are both partly metonymic, with *hands* representing an activity, but a difference between them can be detected in their metaphorical uses of *dirty*: in the first, *dirty* simply represents the side effects of hard physical work, but in the second, *dirty* can be linked to a conceptual metaphor: VIRTUOUS IS CLEAN; NOT VIRTUOUS IS DIRTY.

METONYMY AND METAPHOR

Although some idioms are both metaphorical and metonymic, there are important differences in kind between metaphor and metonymy. Traditional linguists would say that at the heart of each metaphor is a **similarity** drawn between one entity and another: the entities themselves are separate and usually unrelated, and they represent different kinds of thing. In conceptual metaphor theory, this would be expressed in terms of correspondences between two entities which represent two different domains. In both cases, the topic and vehicle, or target and source, remain essentially separate.

In contrast, at the heart of each metonym is a **closeness** rather than a similarity or correspondence (some scholars refer to this closeness as

contiguity). The metonym is an integral part of the entity that it is used to refer to, or vice versa, or is closely connected to it by association: the two elements in a metonym are essentially part of a single thing, and belong to the same domain. The metonym either picks up on one component or connected feature in order to name the whole – or else picks up the whole to refer to a part.

The difference can be seen by comparing the use of *head* in *sixty head of cattle* and *the head of the organization*. The first is a metonym where whole cattle are referred to in terms of a body part (perhaps the part that is simplest to count): heads and cattle are part of the same entity. The second is a metaphor, relating to a metaphorical analogy, or a conceptual mapping, between an organization and a body: organizations and bodies are separate kinds of entity, though there are parallels between them which can be drawn consistently. Lakoff and Johnson (2003. 266) give an example based on time/space, comparing *San Francisco is a half hour from Berkeley* with *Chanukah is close to Christmas. A half hour* is metonymic, referring to a distance which it takes half an hour to travel; *close to* is metaphorical.

Kövecses (2002: 146) describes Gibbs's 'is like' test to distinguish metaphor from metonymy. If one thing can be said to 'be like' another, then it is a metaphor. If it would be nonsensical to say this, then it is a metonym. For example, it is possible to say *the head of an organization 'is like' the head of a body*, but it would be meaningless to say *heads of cattle 'are like' cattle*: rather, we would simply say *heads of cattle 'stand for' cattle*. Gibbs's examples are from American English contexts:

The **creampuff** was knocked out in the first round of the fight.   (metaphor)

We need a new **glove** to play third base.   (metonymy)

'The boxer is like a creampuff' works: 'the third baseman is like a glove' does not. Parallel examples, drawn from BoE, are:

She fell head over heels in love with a man who has turned out to be a real **rat**. (metaphor)

He is the **brains** behind the outfit.   (metonymy)

Metonymy and metaphor also have fundamentally different functions. Metonymy is about *referring*: a method of naming or identifying something by mentioning something else which is a component part or closely or symbolically linked. In contrast, metaphor is about understanding and interpretation: it is a means to understand or explain one phenomenon by describing it in terms of another.

Finally, we should point out that although metonymy and metaphor are generally distinguished, some scholars see them as a single phenomenon and consider metaphor as a kind of metonymy, or metonymy as a form of metaphor. We will not discuss this viewpoint further, except in the context of the experiential basis of metonymy: see below.

SYSTEMATIZING METONYMY

Cognitive approaches to metonymy argue that, like metaphor, metonymy is conceptual in nature:

> Metonymic concepts structure not just our language but our thoughts, attitudes, and actions.
>
> (Lakoff and Johnson 1980/2003: 39)

Metonymic processes are shown to be systematized according to the kind of relationship between the metonym and its meaning, just as metaphorical processes can be systematized according to the conceptual mappings that underlie metaphorical relationships.

Kövecses and others use the terms **vehicle entity** and **target entity** in analysing metonyms. The vehicle entity is the word or phrase which is being used metonymically, while the target entity is the intended meaning or referent. Hence

Vehicle entity	Target entity
hands	workers
the Crown	the monarchy
plastic	credit cards
threads	clothes
wheels	vehicle
bricks and mortar	a house/building
a roof over one's head	place to live

Their terms here can be compared to their use of *source domain* and *target domain* for metaphors – metonyms only relate to one domain – and also to the use of *vehicle* in traditional frameworks for metaphor analysis (see Chapter 1).

A very basic, general metonym is THE PART FOR THE WHOLE, as in the use of *hands* to refer to workers. (Conceptual metonyms are conventionally written in this way, mentioning the vehicle entity first and target entity second: this contrasts with the formulation of conceptual metaphors such as ARGUMENT IS WAR, where the target domain is mentioned first and source domain second.) THE PART FOR THE WHOLE itself subsumes other more specialized metonyms, and Lakoff and Johnson draw attention to one, THE FACE FOR THE PERSON, as in *we need some new faces around here* (their example). THE PART FOR THE WHOLE metonym is reversible to THE WHOLE FOR THE PART, as in *England scored just before half time*.

Some further metonyms which Lakoff and Johnson list, along with their examples, are as follows (1980/2003: 38–9):

PRODUCER FOR PRODUCT

He bought a *Ford*.

He's got a *Picasso* in his den.

OBJECT USED FOR USER

The *sax* has the flu today.

The *buses* are on strike.

CONTROLLER FOR CONTROLLED

Nixon bombed Hanoi.

Napoleon lost at Waterloo.

INSTITUTION FOR PEOPLE RESPONSIBLE

You'll never get the *university* to agree to that.

I don't approve of the *government's* actions.

THE PLACE FOR THE INSTITUTION

The *White House* isn't saying anything.

Wall Street is in a panic.

THE PLACE FOR THE EVENT

Let's not let Thailand become another *Vietnam*.

Remember *the Alamo*.

We can begin to categorize the conceptual metonyms in some of our earlier examples:

Vehicle entity	Target entity	Conceptual metonym
the Crown	the monarchy	THE PART FOR THE WHOLE
threads	clothes	THE MATERIAL FOR THE OBJECT
dish	form of prepared food	THE CONTAINER FOR THE CONTENTS
bricks and mortar	a house/building	THE MATERIAL FOR THE OBJECT
a roof over one's head	place to live	THE PART FOR THE WHOLE
glass, cup, etc.	(its contents)	THE WHOLE FOR THE PART

Some of these metonyms are in fact more complex, with a further layer of metonymic meaning, just as in the case of *plastic* which refers to both credit cards and the system of paying by credit. When we refer to *a roof over one's head*, we are referring to a home, not just a physical building. When we use *hands* to refer to workers, we are referring to people in terms of the work they produce, or traditionally produced, by using their hands. Similarly, *a fresh pair of legs* is used to refer to a substitute soccer player, or *brains* to refer to someone who works with or is noted for their intellect: the body part which has been selected as vehicle entity is conventionally associated with a particular skill, activity, function, or interest factor of the person. The target entity, however, may be the skill, activity, function, or interest factor, rather than the person. See Kövecses (2002: 207–210) for a detailed discussion of metaphors and metonyms which involve *hand*.

In the case of *Crown*, where the target entity is the institution of monarchy, we can detect the broad metonym THE PART FOR THE WHOLE, and a more delicate one, THE CEREMONIAL REGALIA FOR THE INSTITUTION. *Crown* is being used symbolically, and Lakoff and Johnson argue that symbols – in particular, cultural and religious symbols – are essentially metonymic in nature. We will look further at symbols in Chapter 9.

Lastly, an interesting and important pair of conceptual metonyms is EFFECT FOR CAUSE and its reverse CAUSE FOR EFFECT: these, like THE PART FOR THE WHOLE and THE WHOLE FOR THE PART, are very general. One of Kövecses' examples of EFFECT FOR CAUSE is *a slow road* (2002: 154): *slow* refers to journey speeds, but stands for slow-moving traffic on the road. An example of CAUSE FOR EFFECT is *it's a long/ difficult/easy road* to refer to kinds of journey: *road* is metonymic and stands for the journey. The whole notion of cause and effect is tied up with the attribution of responsibility for actions and events, and it is particularly interesting in any exploration of ideological and evaluative aspects of texts. As Lakoff and Johnson point out:

> Nixon himself may not have dropped the bombs on Hanoi, but via the CONTROLLER FOR CONTROLLED metonymy we not only say 'Nixon bombed Hanoi' but also think of him as doing the bombing and hold him responsible for it.
>
> (Lakoff and Johnson 1980/2003: 39)

THE EXPERIENTIAL BASIS OF METONYMY

We referred briefly in Chapter 3 to observations that conceptual metaphors may have an experiential basis: for example, MORE IS UP/ LESS IS DOWN from the sizes of heaps, and ANGER IS HEAT from physiological sensations associated with feeling angry. Lakoff and Johnson see metonyms too as having an experiential basis. They comment that this basis is more obvious

> since it usually involves direct physical or causal associations. The PART FOR WHOLE metonymy, for example, emerges from our experiences with the way in which parts in general are related to wholes . . . THE PLACE FOR THE EVENT is grounded in our experience with the physical location of events.
>
> (Lakoff and Johnson 1980/2003: 39–40)

It has also been suggested that conceptual metaphors may in turn derive experientially from metonyms, or have developed through metonymy. Kövecses explains this as follows:

> The 'body heat produced by anger' can be viewed as a metonymy: BODY HEAT FOR ANGER. Thus, we have the following chain of conceptualization: ANGER

> produces BODY HEAT (metonymy); BODY HEAT becomes HEAT (generalization); HEAT is used to understand ANGER (metaphor). The metaphor ANGER IS HEAT is a case where the source domain of heat emerges from the target domain of anger through a metonymic process.
>
> (Kövecses 2002: 156–157)

Embedded within this is the metonym EFFECT FOR CAUSE: body heat is the effect, anger is the cause. It is the *effect* which gives rise to the metaphor.

Another metaphor conceptualizes relationships in terms of physical proximity (*a close relationship*, *inseparable*; *drift apart*, *break up*, etc.). The experiential basis is fairly clear, and we can link it to a metonym of causation. However, in this case, we might argue about which part of the metaphor relates to CAUSE in the metonym, and which to EFFECT. Is it that physical closeness causes emotional closeness, and physical distance causes emotional distance? Or is it the other way around, with emotional closeness leading to physical closeness, and emotional distance to physical distance? Or both?

SUMMARY

We began this chapter by considering different kinds of metonym, and then metonymy in relation to polysemy and to the meanings of words and idioms. We also looked at conceptual or cognitive approaches to metonymy and the kinds of system which have been identified within metonyms. While we have made a distinction between metonymy and metaphor, we have pointed out lexical items which can be seen as both metonymic and metaphorical, and we commented on how experiential metonymic bases have been said to underlie conceptual metaphors.

Metonymy may sometimes seem a less rich and interesting form of figurative language than metaphor. However, although the evaluative and ideological significance of metaphor may be more obvious, there is also significance in the ways in which metonyms are used, why they are chosen, and what kind of metonymic relationship is highlighted (see Chapter 7). Consider, to conclude, the difference between saying that you like Beethoven or the Red Hot Chili Peppers and saying that you like their music; or saying that Britain sent in troops, rather than that the British government did. This is one of the reasons why metonymy is important.

FURTHER READING

Kövecses, Z. (2002) *Metaphor: a Practical Introduction*, Oxford: Oxford University Press. (Chapters 11, 14, and 15.)

Lakoff, G. and Johnson, M. (1980; new edn 2003) *Metaphors we Live by*, Chicago: University of Chicago Press. (Chapter 8.)

5

UNDERSTANDING
METAPHOR

We have said in earlier chapters that metaphor provides us with ways of explaining, describing, and evaluating; we have also said that metaphor enables us to understand and communicate about abstract and other difficult concepts. But we have not yet addressed the question of how we make sense of metaphorical language, and what mechanisms and processes are involved. Sources for discussion of this topic include psycholinguistics, usually based on experimental data; theoretical discussions in philosophy and semantics; conceptual and cognitive approaches to metaphor, some of which also draw on experimental data; and text-based studies. We will look at these in turn. Discussion will be limited to the understanding and decoding of metaphor, and we will not look at the production of metaphor. In this chapter, we will only consider metaphor in relation to a first or native language: different mechanisms may be involved in understanding metaphor in a foreign language, and we will discuss this briefly in Chapter 6.

METAPHOR AND THE BRAIN

Neurological and psycholinguistic research has indicated that different language functions are associated with different parts of the brain. Early research involved people with brain damage and language disorders: by correlating the location of the brain damage with the nature of the disorder, it was possible to hypothesize about which aspect of language was controlled by which part of the brain. Evidence suggested that, for most right-handed people and many left-handed people, the primary areas for language functions are **lateralized**, in the left hemisphere of the brain. These include Broca's area, particularly associated with the production of speech, and Wernicke's area, particularly associated with comprehension. More recent research supports some degree of lateralization of basic language functions, but has shown that the situation is more complicated: for example, experiments using electrodes or magnetic resonance imaging have found evidence of activity across both hemispheres of the brain.

Other research has suggested that the right side of the brain (in standard lateralizations) is associated with language processes which involve humour, inferencing, irony, and metaphor: all non-literal processes. We can relate this to a more general view of a distinction between 'left-brain' activities (logical, analytical, and rational) and 'right-brain' activities (emotional, expressive, and creative). So one hypothesis is that non-literal language has its own localization and lateralization within the brain. For example, some patients with damage to the right hemisphere of the brain are able to produce and comprehend literal language, but have problems with understanding metaphorical uses.

Nothing, however, is certain, and ongoing research is not conclusive. Furthermore, we have already seen that there are different kinds of metaphor: creative and conventional. If the hypothesis that metaphor processing is lateralized is correct, then it is possible that creative and conventional metaphors are processed differently. That is, creative metaphors would be partly processed in the right hemisphere of the brain, since the intended meaning is not the same as the surface meaning, while conventional metaphors would be processed just like literal meanings, in the left hemisphere. Note that, curiously, when we process conventional metaphors, we may still have residual mental images which relate to the surface meaning of the metaphor, as opposed to its intended meaning: cognitive theorists have made observations about this, and we will discuss them later in this chapter.

METAPHOR AND LANGUAGE ACQUISITION

The ability to understand and use metaphor is sometimes referred to as **figurative** (or **metaphoric**) **competence**, and in this section we look at how it develops in children as they acquire language. We can assess figurative competence by considering how far a child recognizes that the intended meaning of a stretch of language is not its literal meaning, and interprets it metaphorically. It would obviously be unreasonable to expect very young children, capable of producing only very simple one- or two-word utterances, to have any understanding at all of what metaphor is. Most studies investigate children no younger than three, and many studies have focused on children of school age and above.

Generally, children seem to have acquired figurative competence somewhere between the ages of ten and twelve, and to have begun to acquire it by the age of five or six; however, children up to the age of eight or so are likely to produce literal interpretations of metaphorical language, or inappropriate non-literal interpretations. It is difficult to be more precise, since individual children develop linguistically at different rates. Findings from research studies are variable too, partly because of differences in the kinds of task or the kinds of metaphor to which the child informants are asked to respond. In general, young children find it easier to understand explicit similes than metaphors, where similarity or analogy is implicit. However, even very young children are capable of accessing imaginary worlds – they follow stories, and understand what it means to pretend and play. It has been argued that this ability to deal with the unreal is an early form of figurative competence: a pre-figurative competence, perhaps.

Some of the problems which children have with linguistic metaphor arise from their lack of knowledge of the lexicon and of the world. They may know few or no idioms, and they are unlikely to engage in abstract thought. So they may simply not know enough in general to process metaphors, even though they may recognize that a literal interpretation does not make sense. For example, an investigation reported by Ellen Winner (1988: 39ff.) and carried out by Winner, Rosenstiel, and Gardner, asks children about

> After many years of working at the jail, the prison guard had become **a hard rock** that could not be moved.

Some six-year-olds could not interpret it; some assumed the rock referred to prison walls, or thought it meant that the prison guard was very strong and physically hard (another meaning of *hard*, though not the one meant here); and others produced a magical explanation, with the guard being turned into a rock. Some eight-year-olds also produced inappropriate interpretations, although nearly a third of them interpreted the text as referring to the guard's feelings or behaviour. Interestingly, Winner reports that even where informants misunderstood the exact meanings of metaphors, they often recognized whether a metaphor had a positive or negative evaluative orientation.

Most children develop figurative competence in due course along with other cognitive and linguistic abilities. A failure to do so can be considered a dysfunction, and it is symptomatic of particular conditions. For example, one characteristic of some forms of autism, including Asperger's syndrome, is an inability to interpret metaphors, irony, and other non-literal language: this in turn leads to difficulties with conventional social interaction. A 2004 publicity advertisement for the National Autistic Society draws attention to this by listing a number of idioms (*All thumbs, two left feet, [. . .] every cloud has a silver lining, eyes in the back of your head*) and then commenting 'How can someone with autism trust people when all they do is lie?' A novel by Mark Haddon, *The Curious Incident of the Dog in the Night-time* (2003), is a first-person narrative by a teenager with Asperger's. An important theme is his complete honesty, his hatred of lies, including 'social' lies, and his literal use of language and understanding of language. He discusses metaphor:

These are examples of metaphors

[. . .] He was the apple of her eye.
They had a skeleton in the cupboard.
We had a real pig of a day.

[. . .] I think it should be called a lie because a pig is not like a day and people do not have skeletons in their cupboards. And when I try to make a picture of the phrase in my head it just confuses me because imagining an apple in someone's eye doesn't have anything to do with liking someone a lot and it makes you forget what the person was talking about.

(Haddon 2003: 19–20)

It is interesting to consider this perspective in the light of the following discussions of metaphor in relation to truth.

UNDERSTANDING METAPHOR: TRADITIONAL VIEWS

Turning to theories of how people make sense of metaphors, we will look first at traditional views. These largely developed within philosophy – more specifically, the philosophy of language – and semantics, and they predate the work on conceptual metaphor by Lakoff and colleagues. There are important implications to considering metaphor through philosophy, since a major concern has been with truth and logic, including the truthfulness and logic of utterances. This leads to an interest in literal and non-literal meanings, and the extent to which they are 'truthful'.

If we take sentences or utterances such as *apples are fruit, fire burns, water is a colourless liquid*, we can show them to be literally true as propositions, since they represent real states of affairs. Literal linguistic truth corresponds to truth in the world. Conversely, *apples are not fruit, fire does not burn, water is not a colourless liquid* can be shown to be false (we are discounting special contexts such as 'water is not a colourless liquid if you mix it with ink'). In general, utterances which conflict with literal truth, or real-world truth, are seen as problematic. They might result from a deliberate intention to deceive: someone who had knowingly committed a crime might well say 'I did not do it' in order to avoid punishment. However, it would be wrong to say that all utterances which are not literally true are false, wrong, or lies, and metaphor is a case in point.

Some major developments in twentieth-century semantics have resulted from explorations of apparently 'untrue' utterances where there is no intention to deceive or lie. For example, pragmatics in general and speech act theory in particular have explored utterances such as 'Can you pass the salt?' and 'I name this ship Argo', where the first is a request, not a question about ability, while the second is not a simple statement of fact, since by uttering the words the speaker actually performs the act of naming the ship. Other examples of strictly 'untrue' utterances include ironic ones and apparently irrelevant remarks: in both cases, the speaker intends the utterance to be meaningful in context. So in each of the pairs

Can you lend me twenty quid?
I'd love to.

> When are you going to finish that essay?
> Nice weather, isn't it?

the second utterance has a meaning which is not identical with its literal meaning but which is not untrue and irrelevant. These are cases of a gap between **sentence meaning** and **utterance meaning**. That is, there is a gap between the surface meaning and the intended meaning, and so a gap between the meaning of the linguistic form in abstract and its meaning in context.

This, then, is how metaphor fits in, as an example of another kind of gap between sentence meaning and utterance meaning. It becomes another problem to investigate in relation to truth and language: a very old topic, in fact, as Aristotle discussed metaphor in the fourth century BC. There are of course many theories and models of metaphor within the philosophy of language; here, however, we will look at just two, very broad, approaches to the question of how we understand metaphorical language.

In the first of these approaches, metaphor is considered as a kind of **substitution** or **transfer**. This fits with the etymological meaning of the word *metaphor* itself, 'transfer': in compound words, the Greek prefix *metá-* often conveys an idea of change, and *-phor* is from a Greek verb *phérein* 'to carry, bear'. The process of understanding metaphor consists of recognizing that a particular word or expression is polysemous and being used with a secondary metaphorical meaning, rather than its literal meaning. This secondary meaning *substitutes* for another word or expression with a literal meaning. In

> We used to **thrash** all the teams in the Keith Schoolboy League. We had a great squad and no-one could touch us.
>
> (BoE)

the metaphorical meaning of *thrash* substitutes for a more literal word such as 'defeat': *thrash* has another, literal, meaning, 'hit'. This can be expressed more schematically:

Word A   has literal meaning **A**
Word B   has literal meaning **B1**
          has metaphorical meaning **B2**
Metaphor: **B2 is substituted for A**

This view means that we have to consider B as polysemous. However, the metaphorical relationship and substitution is between B2 and A, and we do not need to establish any further connection between B1 and B2. Note that the treatment of polysemous words in current monolingual dictionaries seems to suggest a substitution view of metaphor: metaphorical senses are treated separately from literal ones, but their metaphoricity is usually left implicit and not explained or labelled.

In the second approach, metaphor is considered as a **comparison**. When a metaphor is used, it implies a similarity between the topic and vehicle of the metaphor, and is a shorthand way of saying that the vehicle 'is like' the topic. The process of understanding metaphor is one of recognizing that it is a comparison, what the similarities are, and how the vehicle is relevant to the topic. In the 'thrash' example, the metaphor implies an underlying statement 'winning a game easily is like hitting one's opponents': understanding the metaphor requires us to understand how and why winning a game is like a physical attack. This can be expressed schematically as:

Word A; has literal meaning **A**
Word B   has literal meaning **B**
Metaphor: **A is like B**

This view suggests a closer connection between metaphor and simile, and between the different meanings of a word.

We said in Chapter 1 that some linguists regard the distinction between metaphor and simile as more important than others. It might be truer to say that some linguists are more interested in it than others. If you regard metaphors as comparisons, then similes are also comparisons, and it seems relevant to consider similes too. If you regard metaphors as substitutions, then similes are quite different kinds of item: it would seem less relevant to consider simile than it would metonymy and polysemy in general.

This section has presented a very simplified account of just two overarching approaches to a theory of metaphor. There are other approaches, such as Max Black's 'Interaction view' (Black 1993), and ones which combine elements of substitution and comparison, or take into account the degree to which a metaphorical meaning is conventionalized. For example, it is possible to see substitution and comparison approaches as complementary, with a substitution theory fitting better with conventional metaphors, and a comparison theory fitting better with creative ones. So with a context such as

> The news had shocked her: she was very **agitated**.

we directly access – or substitute – a meaning 'upset and worried' for *agitated*, without analysing further its relationship with a literal meaning 'physically shaken or stirred', or considering its etymological connections. But with a context such as

> The news had shocked her: **a whirlwind of emotions blew her hither and thither**.

we need to identify points of similarity between whirlwinds and emotional states, and what the implications are, in order to make sense of it.

METAPHOR AND PRAGMATICS

We mentioned that pragmatics developed through exploring gaps between sentence meaning and utterance meaning. Pragmatics theory itself has tried to take account of metaphor, and one instance of this is in the work of H.P. Grice. Grice suggested that there is a **Cooperative Principle**, or set of conventions or **maxims**, which we follow in conversation. The maxims relate to Quantity (giving an appropriate amount of information), Quality (being truthful), Relation (being relevant), and Manner (being clear). Hearers expect speakers to conform to these maxims: if they do not conform, but obviously breach or **flout** a maxim, hearers have to interpret the flouting, to understand what the speaker really meant. Grice comments on metaphor as a flouting of one of the maxims of Quality, 'Do not say what you believe to be false.' Since a remark such as *You are the cream in my coffee* (Grice's example) is a falsity, the speaker must mean something different: in this case, the speaker is drawing parallels between the addressee and the cream.

Metaphorical language can be seen as breaching other maxims too. Literary metaphor in particular may be unclear or excessively 'informative' or under-informative, flouting the maxims of Manner and Quantity, and requiring readers to work at interpreting the writer's meaning. Metaphors may also breach the maxim of Relation by being irrelevant.

The operation of the maxim of Relation is the focus of **relevance theory**, developed by Dan Sperber and Deirdre Wilson (1995), following Grice's work. This theory sees relevance as the key issue in how we interpret utterances, and it is interested in the mechanisms of how we make use of contextual meaning and make inferences in making appropriate interpretations. The assumption is that the speaker has supplied all the information necessary and relevant for us to understand the speaker's meaning. How does this apply to metaphors? The following example is an edited transcription of informal conversation, drawn from BoE:

> A: She's complaining that she might have an overdraft that she will have to pay back, and she wants to emigrate the day she qualifies.
> B: Well, you've opened up a whole new can of worms here, I think.

If A interpreted B's response literally, it would be irrelevant and nonsensical. A must assume that B means to be relevant and meaningful, and that no further background knowledge is necessary: A therefore interprets it metaphorically, as an evaluation of what A is talking about.

UNDERSTANDING METAPHOR: COGNITIVE APPROACHES

It is not surprising that Lakoff and colleagues take a very different approach to metaphor from those just mentioned. As we saw in Chapter 3, they argue that metaphor is an essential part of human thought, and that metaphors relate concepts, not the lexical items – or utterances – which realize the concepts. It follows from this that metaphor cannot be considered either problematic or aberrant; that it would be pointless to discuss 'truth' and 'falsehood' in relation to metaphor, since our concepts of truth and falsehood are themselves constructed through metaphor; and that it would be equally pointless to analyse metaphors in terms of the relationship between topics and vehicles, since the real relationship is between the underlying concepts, which consists of correspondences and not similarities.

What then, within the cognitive framework, is said about the mechanisms by which we understand metaphor? Although much is theoretical, some has a basis in psycholinguistic experiments and informant testing, and we will begin with this.

It might be assumed by default that literal meaning is psycho-linguistically prior. That is, when we read or hear a word or phrase used metaphorically, we first try to make sense by interpreting it literally: then, when this interpretation fails because it does not fit the context, we try a secondary, metaphorical reading. When we read

> If the Premier had any **backbone** he would stand up and say 'I won't have this'.
>
> (BoE)

we first interpret *backbone* in its literal meaning of 'spinal column'. This, however, does not make sense: everyone has a spinal column. At this point, we reject the literal reading for a conventional metaphorical one, 'courage and determination', which fits satisfactorily, taking into account the points of correspondence between backbones and courage or determination. This process of trial and error would, like linguistic processing in general, happen instantaneously and subconsciously, but it would still be a two-stage process and should therefore take longer than the processing of literal, straightforward meanings (*if the Premier had any courage* or *the evolution of the mammalian backbone*) – according, at any rate, to the default assumption.

However, psycholinguistic experiments have indicated that this is actually not the case. The processing of metaphors and other non-literal usages does not normally take any longer than the processing of literal ones, and is not normally any more difficult or problematic. (We should exclude from consideration here the special cases of complex, highly stylized literary metaphors, such as *that dolphin-torn, that gong-tormented sea*).

One scholar particularly associated with the cognitive approach and with investigations of the psycholinguistic processing of non-literal language is Raymond Gibbs. He makes a crucial point about the ease with which we understand metaphor, metonymy, irony, and other non-literal language ('tropes', in his terms):

> Speakers can't help but employ tropes in everyday conversation because they conceptualize much of their experience through the figurative schemes of metaphor, metonymy, irony, and so on. Listeners find tropes easy to understand precisely because much of their thinking is constrained by figurative processes.
>
> (Gibbs 1994: 253)

Gibbs, often in collaboration with other scholars, has conducted a series of experiments into the processing of metaphorical idioms: for example, recording the reaction times of informants encountering expressions such as *let the cat out of the bag* and *spill the beans*. Results indicated that the default interpretations were actually the idiomatic meanings, not the literal ones. In fact, when informants were given examples with literal uses of the same expressions, they took longer to process and interpret them than the idiomatic equivalents.

This suggests that in encountering a context such as

they were getting dinner ready when Jack spilled the beans

we would assume that *spilled the beans* meant 'revealed a secret'. If the following context made it clear that Jack had actually dropped vegetables, we would have to backtrack and re-interpret accordingly. From a psycholinguistic point of view, it suggests that idioms are stored in the mental lexicon as complete linguistic units along with their meanings, and are not normally interpreted word by word.

Evidence suggests that conventional idiomatic and metaphorical meanings are processed directly. However, there is also evidence that, if different informants are asked for any mental images of the meta-phorical content, they are not only able to describe these images but there is remarkable consistency between them. For example, when Lakoff asked (American) informants about the images that they had of *spilling the beans*, the general view was that the beans were uncooked and in a container about the size of the human head, that the spilling was accidental and not deliberate, and that the beans were widely dispersed and difficult to retrieve (see Lakoff 1987: 446ff.). In our experience, British informants – mainly undergraduate students – tend to have images of baked beans in a can, but the images are still consistent, and so may simply represent a subcultural variation.

METAPHOR, EXPERIENCE, AND NEURAL MAPPING

We referred in Chapters 3 and 4 to the experiential basis of metaphor which Lakoff and Johnson have described, such as ANGER IS HEAT relating to physiological changes and MORE IS UP relating to the sizes of heaps, while KNOWING/UNDERSTANDING IS SEEING reflects how much of our knowledge is derived from vision. The metaphors AFFECTION IS WARMTH and AFFECTION IS CLOSENESS can be attributed to the physical sensation of warmth or actual physical closeness which arises when one person holds another as an expression of caring and affection: lexical realizations include expressions such as *warm regards* or *a close friendship*. A metaphor PURPOSES ARE DESTINATIONS is attributed to the fact that people go to particular places in order to acquire or achieve particular things: lexical realizations include *arrive*, *reach*, *goal*, and *go to great lengths to* . . . Many other conceptual metaphors have been explained in this way, either by Lakoff and Johnson themselves, or by other scholars working within the same framework.

From this, it can be argued that we acquire metaphorical conceptualizations through our experiences in early life. For example, when we are held as babies by our parents, we learn to associate affection with warmth and closeness, or when we are taken to a particular place to get a particular thing, we learn to associate purposes with destinations. The hypothesis developed by Christopher Johnson (see Lakoff and Johnson 1999: 48) suggests that we first equate or 'conflate' the two concepts, then later learn to differentiate them, and to separate the two domains. (Note that this relates to the acquisition of metaphorical *concepts*, rather than metaphorical vocabulary items.)

Lakoff and Johnson take the argument further:

> Metaphor is a neural phenomenon. What we have referred to as metaphorical mappings appear to be realized physically as neural maps.
>
> (Lakoff and Johnson 2003: 256)

They suggest that when we make the physical association between affection and warmth, the part of the brain which deals with emotion and the part which deals with temperature are activated simultaneously. As a result, the two parts develop neural connections, and there is thus an actual neural structure for the AFFECTION IS WARMTH metaphor. They imply that there are similar mappings with other conceptual metaphors which originate in basic human experiences, and say:

> You don't have a choice as to whether to think metaphorically. Because metaphorical maps are part of our brains, we will think and speak metaphorically whether we want to or not.
>
> (Lakoff and Johnson 2003: 257)

This view is radical. However, it remains a hypothesis, and it is difficult to see how it can be tested methodically at the present time.

BLENDING THEORY

The final aspect of the cognitive approach to be considered is more abstract. **Blending theory** originated in the late 1980s with work by Gilles Fauconnier and Mark Turner (who co-wrote a book on literary metaphor with George Lakoff). It tries to explain what happens when we process metaphors, including the inferences that we make, by means of a complex, dynamic model.

An important part of blending theory is the concept 'mental space'. As a person processes a piece of language, he or she creates a 'space' in the mind. Into this space go all the pieces of information and conceptual knowledge that are needed to process the ideas contained in that bit of language. This will not be *everything* that is known, but only what is relevant to the context.

Blending theory identifies four spaces in relation to the processing of metaphor, which can be represented as follows (after Grady *et al.* 1999):

```
                generic
                space
input                       input
space 1                     space 2
                blended
                space
```

The two input spaces contain the features that characterize target and source domains, while the generic space contains the general features which are common to the two input spaces. In the blended space, the data from the other spaces *blends* together: the output of this space is the meaning of the metaphor.

We can see how this would work with the 'backbone' example:

If the Premier had any **backbone** he would stand up and say 'I won't have this'.

(BoE)

One input space would contain data relating to human behaviour and actions: relevant here is the kind of behaviour and mental attitude needed when difficult action has to be undertaken. The other input space would contain data relating to spinal columns: relevant here is the fact that the backbone is more or less straight and vertical when a person is standing up and in a physical position to take action (irrelevant, hidden features are its structure or position when someone is lying down). There would be mappings between the two spaces, as between target and source domains. The generic space would contain data relating to the features common to the input spaces: here it could crudely be stated as ability to take action. The blended space blends data from the other spaces, to generate a meaning to do with having a quality that keeps you steady and firm when you prepare to take action. This is a simplified analysis, but broadly represents the different elements involved.

A significant feature of blending theory is that both source domain and target domain actively contribute to the blend and eventual meaning: the blend is dynamic. This contrasts with simpler analytical models where contributions to metaphorical meaning go in one direction, from source to target, or vehicle to topic. Supporters of blending theory argue that it provides a much more sophisticated way to analyse complex and creative metaphors; detractors argue that it is too complicated to apply.

UNDERSTANDING METAPHOR: TEXT-BASED APPROACHES

We could characterize the approaches so far as being largely interested in constructing models and theories to explain how people make sense of metaphor – even those which are based on experimental data, or take context into account, as relevance theory does. In the final part of this chapter, we look at approaches which are primarily interested in describing language, rather than constructing theories, and which analyse authentic text data in order to explain how metaphorical meaning is reached.

Corpus linguistics makes use of large quantities of texts, stored on a computer, to analyse the lexis and grammar of a language. Words and phrases are retrieved in multiple contexts, which makes it easy to observe their typical behaviour. Corpus data provides statistical evidence for the relative frequency of different meanings, and what kinds of text they occur in. For example, 70 per cent of occurrences of *attack* represent physical assaults, while less than 20 per cent are metaphorical and refer to arguments and criticism: the commonest text source for these metaphorical uses is print journalism, and they are not especially common in spoken interaction. Corpus data shows that there is often little or no evidence of literal meanings of expressions such as *spill the beans* or *can of worms*: over 99 per cent of examples of *spill the beans* are metaphorical, as are all examples of *can of worms*. This suggests that people are likely to be predisposed to expect metaphorical, not literal, uses, and it supports the psycholinguistic findings which we reported above, where informants took longer to interpret literal uses than idiomatic or metaphorical ones: literal uses are aberrant and therefore unexpected.

Frequency is only one aspect of linguistic behaviour, and corpus linguists also make observations about the collocational and phraseological patterning of different words, or different meanings of a word. Literal and metaphorical meanings are often associated with different clusters of collocates and different phraseologies: *gold*, *diamond(s)*, *ruby/rubies*, *sapphire(s)* co-occur with the literal meaning of *jewel*, while *real*, *hidden*, and *glittering* co-occur with metaphorical uses. Even when literal and metaphorical meanings have collocates in common, there are often some other lexical or structural distinctions: *a precious jewel* is more likely to be metaphorical than literal, but the plural form *precious jewels* is more likely to be literal.

Corpus linguists use data like this to demonstrate that different meanings are normally associated with different patterns and different frequencies in text: ambiguity is rare, because the context shows clearly which meaning is being used. This applies to individual polysemous items such as *attack* and *jewel*, or idioms such as *spill the beans*: it also applies to utterances such as *Sam is a pig*, since the context makes it obvious whether the discussion relates to a person or an animal, and whether the remark is therefore a metaphorical evaluation or a literal statement of fact. Because context distinguishes meanings so strongly, discussions of ambiguity or of literalness and metaphoricity seem entirely artificial. Conventional metaphors are considered simply to be ordinary uses, with their own characteristic patterns and behaviour; creative, one-off, metaphors are considered as atypical or deviant uses, which can be explained by taking into account what would have been normal patterning and behaviour.

Text analysts, too, are concerned with describing meaning in context, including discoursal and cultural context. How should readers interpret figurative language and its ideological subtext, and what kinds of meaning have been created? The following is a longer version of an example we gave in Chapter 1:

> Further around the Waterford coast, Dunmore East settles snugly between small, chunky sandstone cliffs topped by masses of rambling golden gorse. The main street follows a higgledy-piggledy contour from the safe, sandy cove beside which the east village sits, towards a busy harbour full of the rippled reflections of brightly coloured fishing boats and cradled by the crooked finger of the harbour wall. From here, the ruddy sandstone cliffs make bold ribs around the coast. This is still a very active fishing harbour, but has also cashed in on its undeniable picturesqueness, with self-consciously new thatched houses sneaking in alongside the originals.
>
> (Greenwood et al. *The Rough Guide to Ireland*, 1999: 227)

A text analyst would be interested in the meanings that we construct as readers, for example, from the personifications and metonymies of the village 'sitting', the harbour 'cashing in on . . .', or the new houses 'sneaking in'; and the effect created by *cradled by the crooked finger of the harbour wall*, with a possible dissonance between *cradled* and *crooked*, depending on whether we read *crooked* as an adjective meaning 'bent, awry' with a negative evaluation, or the past participle of the verb *crook* 'form into a hooked shape'. Similarly, with the following example from a novel, which contains an extended simile and personification as well as the conceptual metaphor TIME IS SPACE (the narrator is an elderly woman with heart disease):

> I think of my heart as my companion on an endless forced march, the two of us roped together, unwilling conspirators in some plot or tactic we've got no handle on. Where are we going? Towards the next day.
>
> (Margaret Atwood *The Blind Assassin*, 2000: 83)

The comparison suggests a special relationship between woman and heart because of her disease. They are literally inseparable, of course, but figuratively the heart is represented here as a separate being, tied to the woman only through external forces. As readers, we interpret the comparison as showing the woman's attitude to her disease, although our individual interpretations may well vary. Compare our discussion of fuzzy meanings in Chapter 2; Chapters 7 and 8 will look further at figurative language in text, and its implications.

SUMMARY

This chapter has looked at several quite different approaches to the understanding of metaphor. The most 'scientific' investigate real cases, and use experimental data to describe how the brain processes metaphorical language, and how figurative competence develops in children. The most 'traditional' or 'philosophical' approaches investigate metaphor in relation to truth and word meaning, analysing metaphors through logic. 'Cognitive' approaches investigate metaphor through their argument that thought is fundamentally metaphorical and conceptual. 'Context-based' and 'text-based' approaches investigate how information in the context indicates that language is metaphorical, and what kinds of meaning hearers/readers ascribe to metaphor.

None of the theories associated with these approaches, even if it is supported with external evidence, is definitely right, nor is any definitely wrong or misguided. Modelling what goes on when we think is, after all, very hard, even impossible. Perhaps it is appropriate here, then, simply to consider which approaches (and there are others) seem more plausible or satisfying; and how far they conflict with each other or are compatible.

FURTHER READING

Black, M. (1993) 'More about metaphor', in A. Ortony (ed.) *Metaphor and Thought*, 2nd edn, Cambridge: Cambridge University Press: 19–41. (On his 'Interaction' view of metaphor.)

Deignan, A. (2005) *Metaphor and Corpus Linguistics*, Amsterdam: John Benjamins. (A detailed study of metaphor through corpus data.)

Gibbs, R.W. (1994) *The Poetics of Mind: Figurative Thought, Language, and Understanding*, Cambridge: Cambridge University Press. (A cognitive linguistic approach to metaphor: Chapter 9 deals with the acquisition of figurative competence.)

Goatly, A. (1997) *The Language of Metaphors*, London: Routledge. (Chapter 5 deals with relevance theory.)

Grady, J., Oakley, T., and Coulson, S. (1999) 'Blending and metaphor', in R.W. Gibbs and G. Steen (eds) *Metaphor in Cognitive Linguistics*, Amsterdam: John Benjamins: 104–124. (Explanation and discussion of blending theory.)

Kittay, E.F. (1987) *Metaphor: its Cognitive Force and Linguistic Structure*, Oxford: Clarendon Press. (Detailed discussion, with a traditional approach to metaphor.)

Kövecses, Z. (2002) *Metaphor: a Practical Introduction*, Oxford: Oxford University Press. (Chapters 11, 14, and 15.)

Lakoff, G. and Johnson, M. (1980; new edn 2003) *Metaphors we Live by*, Chicago: University of Chicago Press. (Chapter 8.)

Mahon, J.E. (1999) 'Getting your sources right: what Aristotle *didn't* say', in L. Cameron and G. Low (eds) *Researching and Applying Metaphor*, Cambridge: Cambridge University Press: 69–80. (On Aristotle's discussion of metaphor.)

Searle, J.R. (1993) 'Metaphor', in A. Ortony (ed.) *Metaphor and Thought*, 2nd edn, Cambridge: Cambridge University Press: 83–111. (On the interpretation of metaphor.)

Sperber, D. and Wilson, D. (1995) *Relevance: Communication and Cognition*, 2nd edn, Oxford: Blackwell. (Detailed account of relevance theory.)

Winner, E. (1988) *The Point of Words: Children's Understanding of Metaphor and Irony*, London and Cambridge, Massachusetts: Harvard University Press. (Deals with the acquisition of figurative competence.)

6

METAPHOR ACROSS LANGUAGES

So far, we have been considering metaphor and metonymy in relation to English. In this chapter, we will look at how they work crosslinguistically in other languages and cultures. This has practical importance in relation to language learning and translation, and is also significant in relation to more abstract issues of language, culture, and thought.

FIGURATIVE AWARENESS

We have commented that in normal circumstances we are unaware of the figurativeness of conventional metaphors and metonyms: we simply use them as we would ordinary non-figurative meanings or words. We have also commented that figurative competence in children develops over a period of several years: while very young children can only process literal meanings, children of ten or twelve can generally handle most metaphorical usages in non-literary language. However, this applies to the acquisition of a first language, and not a foreign language. Foreign language learning typically begins at an age when we are already competent with metaphor to a greater or lesser extent in our first language. Furthermore, in learning the vocabulary of another language, we may well notice that items are metaphorical, even if the metaphors are conventional: we may also analyse compound items, and think of their literal, compositional meanings. As our comprehension and production of the other language become automatic, this heightened figurative consciousness is likely to fade until it is no stronger than that of native speakers.

For example, when first learning that the French word for 'potato' is *pomme de terre*, we may analyse it as 'apple of the ground' and think of it as some kind of metaphor; similarly with German *Eintopf* 'stew', which literally means 'one pot' and is metonymic. Further examples of metaphorical and metonymic names of foods include the following:

Metaphors

mille-feuille	French 'thousand leaves': cake made with layers of pastry
Apfel Strudel	German 'apple whirlpool': cake with grated apple etc. rolled up in pastry
linguine	Italian 'little tongues': flat, narrow strips of pasta
burrito	Spanish 'little donkey': tortilla wrapped around meat, beans, or cheese
dim sum	Chinese 'dot hearts': meal/course comprising small portions of different foods

Metonyms

paella	Spanish 'pan': rice dish with chicken, shellfish, and saffron
balti	Urdu 'pail': kind of curry served in a large metal dish

METAPHORS IN OTHER LANGUAGES

One interesting question is the extent to which conventional English metaphors are also found in other languages. To investigate this, we can take some of the words which we discussed in earlier chapters — *fox*, *jewel*, *mountain*, *hollow* — and see whether there are similar uses in French and German. The following gives the translations listed in dictionaries for literal and metaphorical senses of the English words.

English word	Sense	French translations	German translations
fox	'animal'	*renard*	*Fuchs*
	'crafty person'	*un fin renard*	*ein alter/schlauer Fuchs*

jewel	'gem'	*bijou, joyau*	*Edelstein, Juwel*
	'something valuable'	*bijou, joyau, trésor, perle*	*Juwel, Goldstück*
mountain	'large hill'	*montagne*	*Berg*
	'large amount'	*montagne, monceau, tas*	*Berg*
hollow	'not solid'	*creux*, etc.	*hohl*
	'meaningless, false, in vain, vacuous, etc.'	*faux, vain*, etc.	*hohl, innerlich*
		creux	*hohl, leer*

French and German, then, have similar metaphorical expressions for the 'crafty person' sense of *fox*. While both languages have other expressions or words for such a person, just as English does, the metaphorical idea that foxes are wily and deceitful crosses the language–culture barriers. It recurs in other languages too, for example Spanish (*zorra, zorro*) and Italian (*volpe, volpone*): compare the reference in names in the film *The Mask of Zorro*, or Ben Jonson's play *Volpone*. French and German equivalents for literal *jewel* are also used metaphorically, and there are parallel uses for broad synonyms of *jewel*. The translations offered for French include *trésor* 'treasure' and *perle* 'pearl', and for German *Goldstück* 'piece of gold': these can be compared with metaphorical uses of *treasure, pearl, gem, diamond*, and so on in English. In the case of *mountain*, both French *montagne* and German *Berg* are used metaphorically: the other French translations offered for the metaphorical sense mean 'pile' or 'heap'. With *hollow*, translations vary according to collocation, whether we are talking about a hollow laugh, promise, threat, or person. In French, *creux* can be used to suggest meaninglessness: *c'est creux* can mean 'there's nothing in it'; but in other contexts translations such as *faux* 'false' or *vain* 'vain' would be used instead. In German, *hohl* 'hollow' covers a wider range of contexts, and *leer* 'empty' contains a similar metaphorical idea.

Not all metaphorical usages are as obvious as these. Many common verbs in English are highly polysemous, and many of their senses are historically metaphorical, although we do not usually notice this. However, when we learn parallel verbs in other languages, we have to consider overtly whether we can use the same verb in all senses. For example, the French equivalent for literal *run* 'move quickly using one's legs' is *courir*, the German is *laufen* or *rennen*, but different verbs might be used to translate other senses. In contexts such as

> the water is running   (= flow)
>
> the machine is running   (= in operation)
>
> run a business . . .   (= manage)

French would use respectively *couler* 'flow', *marcher* 'walk', or *fonctionner* 'function', and *diriger* 'direct, steer'; German would use *laufen* for water or machines running, but *führen* or *leiten* 'lead' for running a business. Finding out how another language lexicalizes English meanings may increase our sensitivity to the metaphoricity of English, if only momentarily.

It is not surprising that there are parallels between English and French or German: English and German developed from the same language-stock, and English absorbed a lot of French vocabulary items, particularly in the Middle Ages, following the Norman Conquest. Completely unrelated languages may have fewer parallels. Japanese, for example, has similar metaphorical meanings for *fox*, *mountain*, and *hollow*, but not for *jewel* and *run*.

IDIOMS

We saw in Chapter 2 that idioms are institutionalized metaphorical expressions with meanings which are sometimes transparent and sometimes obscure. Just as with metaphorical senses, some idioms have direct translations in other languages, incorporating exactly the same metaphor. For example, *be in the same boat* translates directly into French as *être tous dans la même galère* ('galley'), Danish *være alle i samme båd*, German *sitzen alle in einem Boot*, Italian *essere tutti nella stessa barca*, and Spanish *ser embarcados en la misma nave*. The less transparent idiom *bury the hatchet* translates into French as *enterrer la hache de guerre* and German *das Kriegsbeil begraben*: *hache de guerre* and *Kriegsbeil* both literally mean 'axe of war'.

Other English idioms have direct parallels in terms of meaning and underlying idea, but details differ, as with *kill two birds with one stone*:

Dutch	*twee vliegen in één klap slaan* 'kill two flies with one blow'
French	*faire d'une pierre deux coups* 'make two shots with one stone'
German	*zwei fliegen mit einer Klappe schlagen* 'kill two flies with one blow'
Italian	*prendere due piccioni con una fava* 'catch two pigeons with one bean'
Portuguese	*matar dois coelhos de uma cajadada só* 'kill two rabbits with a single stick'
Spanish	*matar dos pájaros de un tiro* 'kill two birds with one shot'

The English expression *butter someone up* has broad parallels in several other languages:

Dutch	*iemand stroop om de mond smeren* 'spread treacle around someone's mouth'
French	*passer de la pommade à quelqu'un* 'rub ointment on someone'
German	*jemandem Honig um den Mund schmieren* 'rub honey on someone's mouth'
Portuguese	*dar graxa a alguém* 'give shoe polish to someone, polish someone's shoes'
Spanish	*dar jabón a alguien* 'rub soap on someone'

where the last also shares a metaphorical image with English *soft-soap someone*.

In some cases, idioms are peculiar to a single language. *Kick the bucket* is an example: one French dictionary suggests *casser sa pipe*, literally 'break one's pipe', as a translation in terms of register and meaning. But the metaphor is quite different, and they are not true equivalents.

METONYMS IN OTHER LANGUAGES

Conventional metonymic uses in English sometimes have exact parallels in other languages, and sometimes do not. The names of places and buildings are widely used to refer to people associated with those places or buildings: *the White House*, French *la Maison Blanche*, and German *das Weiße Haus* can refer either literally to the official residence of the President of the United States, or metonymically to the President and entourage. Words denoting containers are very widely used to refer to their contents: English *cup*, *glass*, French *tasse*, *verre*, and German *Tasse*, *Glas* can either refer to the objects or have the meanings 'cupful', 'glassful', and so on.

In Chapter 4, we discussed metonyms such as these:

Metonym	Meaning
the Crown	the monarchy
hands	workers
head (of cattle)	(number of) cattle
wheels, motor	vehicle
a roof over one's head	place to live

The following gives their equivalents in French and German, where they exist:

English	French	German
the Crown	la Couronne	–
hands	–	–
head (of cattle)	têtes de bétail	–
wheels, motor	–	–
(have) a roof over one's head	avoir du toit	ein Dach über dem Kopf haben

Even if there are no exact equivalents in French and German, there may be related conventions. The French expression *main d'oeuvre*, literally 'hand of work', is used to refer to a workforce or manpower; and the German words *Handarbeiter* and *Handwerker*, 'manual worker', and *Handlanger*, 'odd-job man', all incorporate the morpheme *Hand* with metonymic reference. The idiom *give someone a hand* has parallels in French *tendre la main* and German *jemand zur Hand gehen*. The German expression *pro Kopf* literally means 'per head', and is used in much the same way as the English expression, with reference to people and also cattle and other animals. However, the colloquial uses of *wheels* and *motor* to refer to a vehicle seem to have no direct parallels at all.

CONCEPTUAL METAPHORS AND OTHER LANGUAGES

Chapter 3 was concerned with conceptual metaphors and the work of Lakoff and Johnson. One interesting aspect of conceptual metaphors is the extent to which they are unique to a particular culture, or shared with other cultures. If they are universal, it suggests something very important about human experience and human conceptualizations of phenomena such as life, emotions, causation, and so on. Conceptual metaphors, of course, link concepts, but crosslinguistic discussions naturally focus on language, and that is what we will do here.

While Lakoff and Johnson themselves mainly refer to examples in English, they make some claims about metaphors which they believe to be universal. For the most part, these are the metaphors where the source domains are basic human experiences: orientational metaphors such as MORE/POWERFUL/SUCCESSFUL/ALIVE IS UP, etc., metaphors relating to anger or affection, and so on. Many English realizations of these metaphors are in colloquial expressions or idioms, and other languages do not necessarily have direct equivalents, as we have seen; however, the important issue is whether other languages do indeed incorporate such ideas.

We can investigate this by looking at some examples in French and German. 'Anger' metaphors in English include expressions such as *see red*, *explode with anger*, and *a fiery temper*. The first two of these have direct parallels in French *voir rouge*, *exploser de rage* and German *rot sehen*, *explodieren*; German also has parallels for *fiery* in *feurig* and *hitzig*, but French would use *violent* instead, reflecting the same conceptualization as English *a violent temper*.

Both languages have orientational metaphors relating to MORE IS UP, LESS IS DOWN. This can be seen with verbs such as French *monter* and German *steigen* 'climb', and French *tomber* and German *fallen*, *sinken* 'fall', which also have the meanings 'increase' and 'decrease'. *Tomber* in French occurs in collocations such as *tomber malade*, *tomber de fatigue* 'fall ill, be dropping (from tiredness)'; *fallen* in German can mean 'be killed', as with English *fall in battle*, and *fallen* and *umfallen* occur in expressions to do with sleep and tiredness, such as *zum Umfallen müde sein* 'to be ready to drop'. French *remonter le moral à quelqu'un* literally means 'raise again someone's morale', and *être aux anges* 'be with the angels' has the same kind of meaning as *walk on air* or *be on top of the world*. In German, *steigen* 'climb' occurs in expressions such as *meine Stimmung stieg* 'my spirits rose'; *Wie auf Wolken gehen* ('go as on clouds') parallels English *walk on air* and *on cloud nine*; and *niedergeschlagen* ('lower-beaten') means 'dejected'.

If we consider less closely-related languages, Japanese also conceptualizes anger in terms of heat, and has orientational metaphors relating to quantity, power, success, happiness, and sadness. In fact, as we commented in Chapter 3, all languages investigated so far draw on UP/DOWN concepts in fairly similar ways. This suggests that, to some extent at least, such metaphorical mappings may indeed be universal.

The situation with other metaphors may be more complicated. One way in which English conceptualizes understanding and opinion is in terms of seeing (*I see*, *insight*, *vision*, *view*, *viewpoint*); another is in terms of holding or touching (*grasp an idea*, *get a handle on*, *put one's finger on*). Parallel metaphors exist in many languages. *Viewpoint* has close equivalents in French *point de vue*, Italian *punto di vista*, Spanish *punto de vista*, and German *Gesichtspunkt*. Both literal and metaphorical senses of *see*, 'perceive with eyes' and 'understand', have correspondences in French *voir*, Italian *vedere*, Spanish *ver*, and German *sehen*. However, these verbs cannot be used to translate all contexts where English *see* 'understand' is used: French *comprendre*, Italian *comprendere*, Spanish *comprender*, and German *verstehen* could well be used instead. Interestingly, these last verbs etymologically embody metaphors in which understanding is conceptualized as a physical activity. The first three derive, like English *comprehend*, from Latin *prehendere* 'seize'; German *verstehen* is a compound of *stehen* 'stand', which corresponds to the literal meaning of *stand* in *understand*, even though in English *understand* has from the earliest times referred only to cognition and not to physical position. With respect to non-European languages, Japanese does not seem to conceptualize understanding in terms of seeing in the same way: there is no parallel polysemy in the Japanese equivalent to *see*. Compare, too, the Native American language Hopi, which makes distinctions through its grammatical system between knowledge based on visual evidence and knowledge based on inference and intellectual reasoning: this could suggest a fundamental separation between Hopi conceptualizations of seeing and knowing.

METAPHOR, THOUGHT, AND CULTURE

We have seen that certain metaphorical analogies recur across a wide range of different languages, perhaps because of their basis in human experience, although we have also seen that the detail of metaphors and their exact realizations in vocabulary may vary between languages, even where those languages are related. We have already discussed the argument by Lakoff and others that the use of metaphor to conceptualize – a metaphorical way of thinking – is a fundamental human cognitive process. We now need to see how all this relates to broader issues of language, thought, and culture.

A key issue concerns the interdependence of language and thought. Is the language of a culture determined by the way in which that culture thinks? If so, a language evolves to reflect and express the experiences of its speakers. But what if the opposite is true, and the thoughts of a culture are determined by its language? In this case, its experiences and its understanding of those experiences are constrained because they can only be expressed in the ways which its language allows. An extreme form of this second view is known as the **Sapir–Whorf hypothesis**.

The Americans Edward Sapir and Benjamin Lee Whorf, who lived in the first half of the twentieth century, are noted for their linguistic work, with an anthropological perspective, on Native American and Mexican languages. Whorf's research in particular drew attention to major differences between languages in the ways in which concepts are expressed – for example, Hopi making grammatical distinctions between kinds of knowledge which English does not. Such systematic distinctions have profound effects on how truth is represented or objects are considered, because language conditions or forces speakers to make those distinctions and to think in those ways. The Sapir–Whorf hypothesis developed out of such observations. Differences between languages enforce differences in thought, it claims; their speakers are likely to view the world and its phenomena very differently; and there will not be enough shared ground between speakers of those languages, so that translation becomes impossible.

Few people now support the extreme form of this hypothesis. One counterargument is that translation is not impossible, even if we need lengthy paraphrases to explain distinctions in meaning. Yet there is clearly an intricate connection between language and thought, and it is equally difficult to support an extreme form of the opposite hypothesis, that language is entirely driven by thought, and that thinking and expression are never constrained by the linguistic forms available in a language.

This is particularly relevant to discussions of conceptual metaphor from crosslinguistic and crosscultural perspectives. We can relate the argument that thought determines language to the evolution of conceptual metaphors, especially where physical objects and experiences provide sources for the lexicalization of abstract concepts: argument being conceptualized as war, anger as heat, success and happiness as up, understanding as seeing, and so on. The metaphors are responses to cognitive and expressive needs. Curiously enough, we can at the same time relate conceptual metaphors to the opposite argument that language determines thought. This is most obvious in the case of 'ontological' metaphors. The normal way in which we think of certain abstract concepts is by means of metaphor, and we draw on the linguistic resources of our language through a process of analogy. Thus as English speakers, part of our understanding of illness now is in terms of war, of knowledge in terms of vision and light, of our minds as if they have physical dimensions, and so on. It is difficult for us to think about them in other ways because the metaphors both construct and constrain our understanding.

In English, one way in which we think about large organizations and how they work is in terms of machines: we talk about *the machinery*, *mechanism*, or *wheels of government*, being *cogs in a machine*, and *wheels within wheels* (after Ezekiel in the Bible). There are similar metaphors in other European languages: French *les rouages du gouvernement*, literally 'the cogwheels/gear wheels of government'; Italian *ingranaggi dello stato* 'the mechanism/clockwork of the state'; and German *die Mühlen der Regierung* 'the mill of government'. But if we think of the case of a pre-technological society with a highly-developed social hierarchy, such as some early societies of the Americas, a machine-based metaphor would have been impossible. (This can be related to Lakoff and Johnson's comments about ARGUMENT IS WAR, that if we had come to conceptualize arguments as dances, we would understand and evaluate arguments very differently.) Do the English metaphors, then, construct our understanding of organizations or simply reflect our experiences of them?

To take another case: organizations are also conceptualized in English in terms of buildings, and we talk metaphorically and metonymically about the *corridors of power*, *smoke-filled rooms*, *back rooms*, *the board room*, *the powerhouse*, and so on. What if in talking about another aspect of an organization or institution, we were to conceptualize it in terms of other kinds of room, such as a store-room, kitchen, cellar, or bedroom? Our uses of such metaphors would be mediated by our knowledge of the usual functions and activities associated with those rooms. However, in the case of the Hopi language and culture, Whorf reported that in spite of a relatively highly-developed architecture, and in spite of buildings being divided into sections used for different purposes, there are (or were, at the time of his research) no different terms for different rooms, but only a single word roughly denoting 'space', found in restricted grammatical structures. With respect to different kinds of building: *house*, *church*, *school*, and so on, all have metaphorical uses in English, but Hopi did not distinguish between different kinds of building. So metaphorical uses which involve rooms or buildings, and draw on the specific characteristics of different kinds of room or building, would not have been possible in Hopi. When we looked at metonymy crosslinguistically, we referred to buildings being used to refer to their occupants or to the associated institutions, and said that there are parallels in other languages. But this metonym appeared not to be possible in Hopi, which conceptually separated occupants from the spaces which they occupy, formalizing a cognitive distinction between places and people.

Looking at metaphor in languages other than English, especially when the languages are very different from English, helps our under-standing of metaphor in general. The very nature of conventional metaphor is that we are normally unaware of its figurativeness; the way it affects meaning and thought is therefore subliminal. But if we are told, say, that in Inuktitut *inuktariwa* can mean either 'killed him' or 'took him as servant', we could well make inferences about power in Inuit society, or about an equation of loss of life and loss of independ-ence; and if we are told that *nakkertok* can mean 'goes fast' or 'goes far', we could make inferences about equations of speed and distance. They seem significant, but are perhaps no more so than conventional English metaphors, such as *slaughter* in 'Manchester United slaughtered Arsenal 6–1' or *long* in 'I travelled for a long time'. See Kövecses (2002: 163–197) for extended discussion of metaphor in languages other than Western European ones.

TRANSLATING METAPHOR

The final sections of this chapter consider implications for the translation of metaphor. Translation is straightforward at times. The same meta-phor may exist in both the source language (or original language) and the target language (or language into which the text is being translated). The following examples are taken from novels in English in BoE:

> He leaned against the tiled wall and considered the pointlessness of further pursuit. Enrico was too good, an old **fox**, cunning. He was giving nothing away.

> 'I wish I had heard it,' said the Admiral. He refilled Jack's glass and said, 'Your surgeon sounds a **jewel**.' 'He is my particular friend, sir: we have sailed together these ten years and more.'

As we have seen, French, German, and Japanese all have conventional metaphors which more or less correspond to that of English *fox*. Similarly, a translator could feel reasonably confident that a French or German reader would understand *bijou/joyau* or *Edelstein/Juwel* in much the same way as an English reader would understand *jewel*. However, there are sometimes differences in connotation or usage which affect the meaning. For example, *seed(s)* is used metaphorically in phraseologies such as *seeds of doubt*, *dissension*, *conflict*, *success*, etc. In many languages, parallel uses of *seed(s)* can be used either of good or bad situations, but in some others, only of good (there may be cultural reasons for this, with crops and plants being regarded entirely positively). Sometimes languages have corresponding metaphors, but they differ in frequency or formality, so a translator might well choose a different form of words: someone translating 'I see what you mean' into German might use the verb *verstehen* 'understand', rather than a metaphorical expression with *sehen* 'see'.

Some metaphors do not translate exactly into other languages, although there may be very similar metaphors which exploit the same underlying concept. It would be appropriate, then, for someone translating

> It proposes no startling changes to **the machinery of government** that has been in place since 1975.

> (BoE)

into French or German to select *les rouages du gouvernement* or *die Mühlen der Regierung*. Another possibility is that source and target languages may both have metaphorical expressions with similar meanings, but the actual metaphors do not correspond. An example is English *invest*, as in 'I've invested a lot of time' (compare the literal use 'I've invested a lot of money'). Since the French equivalent for the metaphorical use is *consacrer* 'devote, consecrate', as in 'j'ai consacré beaucoup de temps', the connotation of the metaphor is different (*investir* and *placer* are equivalents for the literal meaning). There are degrees of correspondence too: French *faire d'une pierre deux coups* and German *zwei fliegen mit einer Klappe schlagen* seem to correspond well enough to English *kill two birds with one stone*. In the case of French *casser sa pipe* and English *kick the bucket*, a translator may feel that the crucial part of the translation is the dysphemistic informality of the idiom, not the image, so that selecting an idiom as translation seems a better way of representing the meaning of an English original than simply using *mourir* 'die'.

In other cases, there is no institutionalized metaphorical equivalent at all, and so the only or best translation would be non-metaphorical. We commented earlier on translations of *run* to refer to flowing water. In English, we can talk of rivers running too:

> We were on a bend in the road and I could see the river, grey with sediment, running swiftly between bare mountains that came down to the river on the opposite side.

(BoE)

If a translator used the equivalent to literal *run* – for example, *courir* rather than *couler* 'flow' in French, or *rennen* rather than *fließen* 'flow' in German – it would seem inappropriately literary, and could even suggest personification of the river, creating an anthropomorphic image, whereas it is ordinary usage in English.

We can further demonstrate translators' choices with examples taken from multilingual versions of European Union debates (this data was generously provided by our colleague, Philip King). The English speaker uses an idiom in the following:

> Mr President, it is time for Europe to **get off the fence** and make clear its support for Taiwan.

The corresponding French and Italian translations are as follows:

> Monsieur le Président, il est temps pour l'Europe de **franchir le pas** et de dire nettement son soutien à Taïwan.

> Signor Presidente, per l'Europa è giunta l'ora di **uscire dal riserbo** e di esprimere con chiarezza il suo sostegno a Taiwan.

The French translation of the idiom, *franchir le pas*, literally means 'cross the step' and is parallel to *take the plunge*; Italian *uscire dal riserbo* 'abandon reticence' is parallel to *drop one's reserve*. Different expressions have been substituted and the tone is maintained, but the meanings are not quite the same. In the following example, the original is French:

> J'aurais tendance à répondre que ce n'est pas en **se mettant la main devant les yeux** que, pour autant, on changera la réalité.

here the metaphor literally means 'putting one's hand over one's eyes'. The Italian translator keeps the same metaphor, but the English one introduces a different one:

> Sarei propenso a rispondere che non è certo **mettendosi la mano davanti agli occhi** che si può cambiare la realtà.

> My answer is that people cannot change reality by **burying their heads in the sand**.

Most of the preceding has concerned conventional metaphor. Creative metaphors in other languages are also interesting; however, they are individual cases which reflect cultural traditions of discourse and text, as well as the metaphorical characteristics and capabilities of different languages. Translators of non-literary texts have to balance the importance of maintaining the rhetorical style of the original against the need to avoid distracting lexical devices by translating word for word. Different protocols again apply to literary texts. Here, translators might well feel that it was important to reproduce the metaphorical choices of the original writer, in order to maintain the imagery of the text, rather than substituting near-equivalent or non-metaphorical expressions. We would, for example, expect a translator of Shakespeare to retain the metaphors of

> To be, or not to be: that is the question:
> Whether 'tis nobler in the mind to suffer
> The slings and arrows of outrageous fortune,
> Or to take arms against a sea of troubles,
> And by opposing end them . . .

Similarly, we accept word-for-word translations of poetry into English, however marked they are or 'un-English' they sound. For example, the Old English poetic metaphor *hronrāde*, referring to the sea, literally translates as 'whale road', and a translation *whale road* seems preferable to simply using *sea*. This is what Seamus Heaney chose to do in his translation of *Beowulf*:

> In the end each clan on the outlying coasts
> beyond the whale-road had to yield to him
> And begin to pay tribute.
>
> (Heaney 1999: 3)

Compare the following opening of the poem 'Romance sonámbulo' ('Somnambular Ballad', 'Sleepwalking Ballad') by the Spanish poet Lorca, who is noted for his striking imagery, and a parallel translation by Merryn Williams:

Verde que te quiero verde.	Green how much I want you green.
Verde viento. Verdes ramas.	Green wind. Green branches.
El barco sobre la mar	The ship upon the sea
y el caballo en la montaña.	and the horse on the mountain.
Con la sombra en la cintura	With the shade at her waist
ella sueña en su baranda,	she dreams on her balcony,
verde carne, pelo verde,	green flesh, green hair,
con ojos de fría plata.	and eyes of cold silver.
Verde que le quiero verde.	Green how much I want you green.
Bajo la luna gitana,	Beneath the gypsy moon,
las cosas la están mirando	things are looking at her
y ella no pueda mirarlas.	and she cannot see them.

(Lorca 1992: 74–75)

This is not completely literal, but it broadly maintains the images and poetic qualities of the original.

SUMMARY

We began this chapter by considering how we have different levels of awareness of figurative language when learning other languages, compared with our first language. We considered cases of equivalents in other languages to metaphors, idioms, and metonyms. We saw that some have direct equivalents, some similar, some parallel (with different metaphorical images), and others no figurative equivalents at all: we also saw that even apparent equivalents may have slight differences in meaning and usage. We considered conceptual metaphors, mainly with respect to whether they were universal or specific to a language/culture. In relating this to broader issues of language, culture, and thought, we discussed how metaphors (and metonyms) indicate differences in viewpoint and understanding, and may constrain it. Lastly, we discussed some practical issues and cases of actual translations of metaphors.

It is, perhaps, appropriate to end by saying that the selection of a translation is not just lexical or semantic, but evaluative and ideological too: switching one metaphor for another may change the reading of the original in significant ways. This means that translators need to be aware of the discourse function of the original metaphor – how it evaluates, and whether it is being used to explain something more clearly, or perhaps to conceal or 'code' the real meaning. These are issues which we will return to in the following chapters.

FURTHER READING

Baker, M. (1992) *In Other Words*, London: Routledge. (Chapter 3 considers the translation of idioms and other figurative expressions.)

Kövecses, Z. (2002) *Metaphor: a Practical Introduction*, Oxford: Oxford University Press. (Chapters 12 and 13.)

Montgomery, M. (1995) *An Introduction to Language and Society*, 2nd edn, London: Routledge. (Chapter 11 introduces the ideas of Sapir and Whorf, and then explores evaluative aspects of language.)

Newmark, P. (1988) *A Textbook of Translation*, London: Prentice Hall. (Chapter 7 deals with literal translation, Chapter 10 with the translation of metaphors, and Chapter 15 with the translation of literature.)

Whorf, B.L. (1956) *Language, Thought, and Reality*, Cambridge, Massachusetts: MIT Press. (A collection of Whorf's papers, to be read selectively, for data on how Hopi and other languages lexicalize and conceptualize the world.)

7

METAPHOR, IDEOLOGY, AND SOCIAL CONTEXT

This chapter, together with Chapters 8 and 9, will shift the focus of this book from background issues to figurative language in context, and we will make detailed reference to actual data. As these three chapters are, in a sense, applied or practical, we feel that it might be useful for you to 'unpack' or interpret some of our examples. We will make some suggestions for practical work as we proceed.

In Chapter 2, we considered metaphor in relation to the meaning of words and phrases and saw that the meaning of a word or phrase is not just the surface or literal meaning. Sometimes, indeed quite often, words can be put together in a text with the intention of putting forward a particular point of view, of trying to persuade a reader or listener that this is *the* point of view. In other words, the text is evaluative in some way or, if you like, it contains an 'ideology'. In this chapter, we are going to explore the notion of metaphor and evaluative language in a variety of domains or contexts. As a starting point, we will look at *upward* 'movement' as opposed to *downward* 'movement' in English. Generally speaking, we see that *up* tends to positive evaluation while *down* tends to negative evaluation. Sometimes, of course, 'upness' can express negative evaluation as in:

Military budgets had continued to **spiral**.

But *spiral* can also be used to indicate downward movement in negative contexts:

Industry had entered a **spiral** of decline.

From our own data, we can illustrate the up/down positive/negative contrast in English with:

M&S **ups** sweetener to £2bn

(*The Observer* (*Business*), 11 July 2004)

This is the headline of an article concerned with negotiations for the take-over of the British company Marks and Spencer. Marks and Spencer are apparently increasing share values (*ups sweetener*) to make the company more attractive financially. Of course, from another point of view, it could be argued that this particular 'upping' reflects negative evaluation in that the *sweetener* might be seen as a kind of bribe. However, it is certainly positive for the shareholders and contrasts with:

Roof falls in on buy-to-let scam

(*The Guardian* (*Jobs and Money*), 6 March 2004)

This refers to an article about alleged losses (*roof falls in*) by investors in a property investment scheme.

In general, then, in Western culture, good things are *up* and bad things are *down*. Lakoff and Johnson give a number of different orientational metaphors which clearly demonstrate the UP/DOWN polar oppositions that exist metaphorically in Western culture (see Lakoff and Johnson 1980/2003: 14–21). In their discussion, they also make the point that such orientational metaphors may not be exactly the same in other cultures. In Chapter 9, we will see how, in metaphor associated with religious belief, this UP versus DOWN contrast was conceived of in terms of Heaven (UP) and Hell (DOWN). In Victorian England, there was a considerable output of evangelical fiction for both adults and children and the authors laid great emphasis on 'good' people going 'up there' to Heaven and 'bad' people going 'down there' to Hell. In fact, poor and hungry people were being constantly urged that their 'reward' would come in heaven. In one such narrative, by Charlotte M. Tucker, *The Green Velvet Dress* (1858), there is a little boy called Tommy.

Tommy is slowly starving and Tucker presents Tommy's future (death) in poem form using the metaphor of *a happy home above*:

> Ne'er will I sigh for wealth,
> Such wealth as coffers can hold:
> Contentment, union and health,
> Are not to be bought for gold!
> The costly treasures I prize
> Are treasures of family love –
> Of **a happier home above**
>> (Tucker 1858/1993: 101)

In other words, money cannot buy happiness (though the fact that it can buy food seems to have been overlooked) and Tommy's reward will come *up there*.

METAPHOR AND POLITICAL NARRATIVE

In a very different, contemporary, context we can again see metaphor being exploited evaluatively. Evaluation or ideology is, for many, usually associated with political beliefs and it is quite true that political parties want to persuade us that their way is the right way. Ideology, however, need not necessarily be thought of in purely political terms. Ideology can be seen as a set of beliefs which provides justification for what people do and say. As such, the social dimension is very important, and language plays a key role in realizing these social and political values. In fact, the notion of social contexts is very useful in describing how language operates in different situations. We will start with the following:

> In Downing Street, it was as if **a hand grenade had landed** in the front hall. Through the next few weeks newspaper front pages were **pockmarked** with the **fallout, a shower of anti-Brown stories** . . .
>
> Campbell and Hunter form the circle of **intimates** who are **Blair's armour**. Brown **wears a similar protective suit**. His most important adviser is Ed Balls . . . Balls was left as the Chancellor's principal political **lieutenant**. He is a disarmingly cheery soul, given much more to laughing than to **dark conspiracies**, but he has created **a fearsome reputation** for himself.
>> (James Naughtie *The Rivals*, 2001: 246)

The writer, James Naughtie, is a respected British journalist and presenter on the BBC's current affairs programme, *Today*. In his book, Naughtie charts the relationship between the British Prime Minister, Tony Blair and the Chancellor of the Exchequer, Gordon Brown. The title of the book, *The Rivals*, is itself metaphorical as it is unlikely to be a coincidence that it is exactly the same as Richard Brinsley Sheridan's famous play, *The Rivals*. Furthermore, the subtitle of Naughtie's work is *The Intimate Story of a Political Marriage*.

The context of this extract is that it claims to be the response by Downing Street (the official residence of the British Prime Minister, and a good example of metonymy) to a biography of Gordon Brown published in 1998. The biography is the work of a political commentator critical of the Prime Minister, Tony Blair. Gordon Brown himself was not quoted in the biography but it was written, it was asserted on the cover, 'with the Chancellor's "full permission"' (2001: 246). So, we have a representation of relationships within this *marriage*. Naughtie is not quoting directly either Blair or Brown but commenting on how the relationship between the two might be viewed given their political history. Allegedly, the two men have an uneasy relationship. In fact, we can view this as a type of ARGUMENT IS WAR conceptual metaphor. The metaphor is extended: it is not just a war metaphor but mainly a nuclear war one.

The nuclear war metaphor is recycled throughout the two paragraphs from which this extract is taken to provide a cohesive account of one view of the two politicians' relationship at this time. We can unpack it as follows:

context the book plus earlier alleged criticism of Brown by supporters of Blair (this criticism is not included in the extract but precedes it)

vehicle nuclear war

topic alleged hostility between the two major politicians and their supporters

grounds the idea of extreme aggression between two powerfully armed opponents

Now, given the above, consider how the metaphor is realized by Naughtie as a metaphorical chain. Let's break it down into its constituent parts:

The book is a **hand grenade**: the book is an explosive device.

Newspaper pages were **pockmarked with the fallout, a shower of anti-Brown stories**: the result of publication of the book was considerable negative evaluation of one of the participants in the media.

Campbell and Hunter, **the intimates**, are **Blair's armour**: one participant had powerful friends/allies to protect him.

Brown had **a similar protective suit** (Ed Balls), Brown's **principal political lieutenant**: the other participant also had a powerful defender, who is, in addition, his main professional adviser.

In sum, this is a mini-narrative and exemplifies well Naughtie's style of writing (not unlike his oral presentation in the media), which carries more than a small degree of irony (see Chapter 8). Admittedly, *intimates* is not overtly a 'war word', but within the context of this text, it is not unreasonable to present it as we have done, that is, as *allies*. Overall, the relationship between literal and metaphorical meaning contributes to an especially effective metaphor. Note particularly the change of focus from *a hand grenade* landing in the front hall to the concept of a shower of radioactive fallout.

There are two other highlighted phrases, and we can see a connection with the war metaphor. Both *dark conspiracies* and *a fearsome reputation* would not be out of place in war history or war narrative. The presence of words like *dark* and *fearsome* is not surprising, given the vehicle, nuclear war. A *conspiracy* is a plot by, usually, a small group of people to overthrow leadership and replace it. The fact that our conspiracy is a *dark* one emphasizes danger and fear. However, even though Ed Balls may not be a *conspirator* he has, apparently, *a fearsome reputation*. In other words, he has caused himself to be regarded in a most frightening and terrible way. Or is Naughtie being ironic here?

METAPHOR AND THE REPORTING OF THE NEWS

In Chapter 3, we discussed the systematization of metaphor. We saw how metaphorical links between concepts may be culture-specific as, for example, Western society's view of ARGUMENT IS WAR. The following examples illustrate this particularly well. We will now look at politics again but this time in the context of the reporting of the news. First, an extract from *The Guardian* puts forward a point of view, apparently held by certain top members of the British Government, of the role of the media over the resignation of British cabinet minister Estelle Morris:

Cabinet attacks media war on Morris

Leading figures in Tony Blair's cabinet suddenly **rounded on** the media yesterday **accusing it** of **hounding a wounded Estelle Morris**, the former education secretary, from office.

(Patrick Whelan *The Guardian*, 25 October 2002)

To *round on* someone means to attack them swiftly and aggressively. The topic of speed and aggression which we can unpack from *round on* is reinforced by the verb *accused*. In other words, it is alleged that the media have done something *wrong* or *bad*, and if that is not enough, the metaphor is extended with the accusation being spelled out in uncompromising terms. They have been *accused* of:

hounding a wounded Estelle Morris.

To *hound* someone means to criticize them continuously, using strongly worded or aggressive language as in:

He was hounded by the press.

The grounds between usage and meaning in the Estelle Morris extract lie in the idea of pursuit by a savage body or group (*a pack of hounds?*: compare the old-fashioned word for a reporter, *newshound*), who are intent on destroying their *wounded* quarry. The inference here is that Estelle Morris's feelings have been deeply hurt and her reputation damaged by the media. *Wound* is itself, of course, part of the vocabulary of the metaphor, ARGUMENT IS WAR.

The point of view of the 'leading figures' above, however, may not be the same as that of others. Equally, *The Guardian* might not share the point of view of other British newspapers such as *The Daily Telegraph* or the *Sun*. It certainly did not, over the issue of Estelle Morris, share the point of view of the *Daily Mail*, a British tabloid newspaper:

So let us **nip one thing in the bud**. Contrary to **Westminster mythology – outrageously spread** by Robin Cook – Miss Morris was *not* **hounded out**.

(Comment *Daily Mail*, 25 October 2002)

In this *Daily Mail* extract, we know that the topic, like *The Guardian*'s, is Estelle Morris's resignation. In assigning responsibility for the resignation, we are given a different point of view. That is, the media are *not* to blame for the resignation. When the *Daily Mail* uses the metaphor *Westminster mythology*, it is as good as saying 'Westminster lies': a body of myths is, after all, a body of false or legendary but widely held notions. Thus, according to the newspaper, 'Miss Morris was *not hounded out*'. It is also interesting how other attitudinal language supports this metaphor. *Outrageously* here means that what Robin Cook has allegedly spread is socially and morally unacceptable, and *spread* itself can be seen as metaphorical. Note also the role of those taking part in the interaction. The 'silent partner', the reader, has been included in the discourse by the *Daily Mail*'s Comment writer. The use of *let us* makes the assumption that writer and readers together will *nip one thing in the bud*.

In Chapter 2, we introduced the notion of idioms as a kind of metaphorical phrase. For a native speaker of English, *nip something in the bud* is straightforward. *Nip* literally means 'give someone a small but possibly painful pinch or squeeze with one's fingers'; *bud* means early growth as in *rosebuds* or *the apple trees are in bud* (closely connected is the use of *budding* in contexts such as 'He's one of our better-known budding actors' or 'She's only eighteen but she's already a budding entrepreneur'). The meaning in the *Daily Mail* report is, however, interpreted from the metaphor that the idiom contains. Here the journalist is urging that the *myth* (lie) that Estelle Morris was *hounded out* (forced out) of office should be quashed now. In other words, 'put an end to this untruth immediately, before it *flowers*'.

Bearing in mind how much more difficult it is to decode some idioms in terms of their literal meanings, we turn again to the discourse of politicians. The incident concerned was reported by *The Guardian* and has to do with the politics, and two of the political figures, of Northern Ireland. The raids referred to were police raids on the offices of the Irish political party Sinn Fein at Stormont Castle, the seat of the Northern Ireland Legislative Assembly: Sinn Fein is the main opposition party to British rule in Northern Ireland. Two Unionist MPs made statements regarding the police action, which put forward their point of view. The Unionists represent the 'loyalist' or pro-British lobby. First, Jeffrey Donaldson, at that time Ulster Unionist MP for Lagan Valley constituency, stated that the raids were

> 'the final nail in the coffin' of Sinn Fein's participation in the government of Northern Ireland.
>
> (Rosie Gowan *The Guardian*, 5 October 2002)

His colleague, the east Belfast Democratic Unionist MP Peter Robinson, was not to be outdone:

> the fact that such a raid [*sic*] has taken place must 'drive a coach and horses through' protestations that Sinn Fein is committed to exclusively peaceful means.

In these extracts, both politicians use an idiom:

the final nail in the coffin

drive a coach and horses through

We observed in Chapter 2 how corpus evidence shows up clusters of variable wordings for idioms, and Jeffrey Donaldson's *the final nail in the coffin* belongs to one of the clusters we cited there. Of the two idioms, the first one is probably less opaque in terms of interpretation. In other words, *the raids* mean the 'death' (another metaphor) or the end of 'Sinn Fein's participation in the government of Northern Ireland'.

The meaning of the second idiom has to do with size and weight. Peter Robinson is effectively saying Sinn Fein's 'protestations' of commitment to rule by peaceful means are flimsy. The fact that the raids were on Sinn Fein offices provides the 'force' (the *coach and horses*) to destroy these 'protestations'. In effect, Peter Robinson is implying that Sinn Fein are lying about their declared commitment to peaceful government. He might as well have used another idiom, *there's no smoke without fire*.

The imagery conjured up by both idioms is a result of language in use to reinforce a particular political ideology. It is significant that they are taken from the social context of political speeches. Both politicians are known for their fundamental but passionate styles of oratory. We can assume that the dramatic use of two very well-known and figuratively very strong idioms would appeal to their political followers.

Interestingly, in the same account of the debate in which Peter Robinson delivered his *coach and horses* image and Jeffrey Donaldson his *nail in the coffin*, we have another evaluation of the same incident. The expression of this point of view carries some of the language of the ARGUMENT IS WAR conceptual metaphor. The speaker is Barbara de Bruin, a leading Sinn Fein politician, who wants Dr John Reid, then Secretary of State for Northern Ireland, to justify the raids:

> But Barbara de Bruin, the Sinn Fein Stormont Health minister, **challenged** Dr Reid to explain why the raids were carried out.
>
> 'This is **a politically inspired ricochet** into the middle of **a highly volatile situation. It Is an attack on** Sinn Fein and the process of change, **it is damaging** to everybody involved in the peace process.'

Note, first, the newspaper's selection of the verb *challenged* to introduce what de Bruin says. A *challenge* can mean a questioning of the truth or the necessity of something; however, it can also mean to issue a dare or give cause to or invite someone to *fight*. A *ricochet* literally refers to a bullet which has been fired and which then bounces off another surface at an angle. The *politically inspired ricochet* means the raids were, allegedly, a result of a deliberate Government decision. The raids, then, were *a bullet that missed its* 'intended' *target* and 'bounced', having a most detrimental effect on the *highly volatile situation* that is the *emotional and dangerous context of Northern Irish politics*. Barbara de Bruin also uses the metaphor to point out that police (British Government) action has seriously *damaged* the democratic structure of the Assembly. In sum, then, the action, from de Bruin's point of view, is:

a ricochet (into **a highly volatile situation**)

damaging

an attack

Ideologically, de Bruin sees the whole Good Friday Agreement (the agreement reached by the political parties of Northern Ireland on

Good Friday 1998) as under threat. In other words, the attack is not only on Sinn Fein but on the peace process itself. For Jeffrey Donaldson and Peter Robinson, on the other hand, the raids demonstrate the undemocratic position of Sinn Fein because the police allegedly found it necessary to search their offices. These are two different 'points of view', and two different 'ideologies'.

The WAR metaphor can contribute to the cohesive structure of newspaper items outside political contexts. Consider the following extract from a report by Mark Townsend:

Alien Invasion: the plants **wrecking** rural Britain

Aliens are taking over the British countryside.

Our rivers are being **choked to death**, our meadows **overrun** and our native species **smothered to the brink of extinction**. And the **invasion** is almost complete.

The first study of its kind into the remarkable spread of non-British plants reveals that more than 80 per cent of Britain has been **infiltrated**.

Virulent 'superweeds' . . . are **conquering Britain** with a speed that has astonished scientists. Practically all of lowland Britain has been **colonised** . . .

(*The Guardian*, 2 February 2003)

Mark Townsend sees Britain's natural flora as being under threat from *invasion* by *aliens*. He looks at Britain's flora, the target, in terms of war, using warlike language such as might also be found within the context of science fiction. This is connoted by the item *aliens*, and associated items such as *infiltrated*, *virulent*, *conquering*, *colonised*. There are resonances here of John Wyndham's classic science fiction novel *Day of the Triffids*, in which the planet Earth is overrun by giant plant-like creatures.

Now, consider this example of metaphor in the reporting of the news. It comes from *The Independent* (14 June 2004):

THE SCAPEGOAT

This refers to the resignation of the Central Intelligence Agency's director, George Tenet, over the issue of weapons of mass destruction and Iraq. In the opening paragraph of this front-page article, Mr Tenet is referred to as:

> the Bush administration's **de facto scapegoat**

The item is used again in the article, with a quote from a former CIA director who apparently said of Tenet:

> He's being pushed out: it's likely he's **the scapegoat**

On page 5 of the same edition of *The Independent*, we have:

> Is CIA director **the scapegoat** for Iraq?

Furthermore, in its leading article for that day (page 30) and on that topic, we read:

> This **cheap sacrifice** offers little solace to those who question the Iraq war

and later:

> If the departure of Mr. Tenet is **a cheap sacrifice** from Mr. Bush's perspective . . .

The *Independent* journalist has used the biblical concepts of the scapegoat and a sacrifice. In contemporary usage, a *scapegoat* ('a whipping boy' or 'fall guy') is someone to take the collective blame for something that, in the eyes of the community, has gone badly wrong. The origins of the term lie in ancient Judaism where a goat was sent out into the desert as a sacrifice. The goat was supposed to carry with it the sins of the community. There is poignancy here, as the Jewish population of Nazi Germany were made scapegoats by Hitler, with the tragic results that we now call the Holocaust. We will return to the metaphors of *scapegoat* and *sacrifice* later on.

METAPHOR AND SPORT

Consider the following headline:

> Must do better, warns **badly wounded Tiger**
>
> (Robert Kitson *The Guardian* (*Sports Supplement*), 5 October 2002)

Animal metaphors are not uncommon in the language of sports reporting or in the naming of teams in different sports. In the United States, the *Chicago Bulls* are a well-known American basketball team. However, the extract above is especially culture-bound. *Guardian* readers who follow rugby football would be able to interpret the evaluation carried by the animal metaphor, since they and the journalist Robert Kitson share a common sporting environment. The readers would recognize the vehicle, *badly wounded Tiger*, and the idea of a large and savage animal that has been badly hurt. The connection or grounds lie in the fact that Leicester City Rugby Football Club's nickname is 'The Tigers'. (You might also want to consider the *must* in the headline. The evaluation contained in the metaphor is given added force by this modal verb: in English, meanings concerned with certainty, possibility, obligation, permission, and volition are traditionally realized by modality.)

Let's look at the metaphor again. The *badly wounded tiger* of the headline is Martin Johnson, the club's and England's captain. He is not physically hurt, as Estelle Morris was not physically hurt, in our earlier, political metaphor. Rather, the *wound* is shared with his colleagues; it is a collective wound. This club had been at the top of the English rugby premier league for some years, but had not been performing well since the start of the new season. In this report, both Robert Kitson and Martin Johnson evaluate the club metaphorically as a *badly wounded tiger*. In other words, their reputation as a top sporting side has been damaged.

The importance of the metaphor *wounded* in both contexts, the political and the sporting, lies in the fact that metaphorical language is not necessarily context-bound. It is a 'shared' item within the wider discourse of journalism. The *Guardian* reader will take on board instantaneously and subconsciously the relationship between the different elements of:

wound   (vehicle)

being badly hurt   (topic)

notions of fierceness/savagery   (grounds)

be it

Context 1: . . . accusing it of hounding a **wounded** Estelle Morris or

For readers interested in both politics and rugby, the ability to interpret and adapt their interpretations to context will not be problematic. The shared knowledge that the readers possess allows them the ability of interpretation whether it is politics or sport or both. The recognition and interpretation of the metaphor is part of the shared knowledge that exists here between the journalists and their readers, what Kövecses (2002: 207) calls 'conventional knowledge'.

Moving on to a different sport, consider the headline below:

Anfield winter of discontent as fans turn on the boss

(John Edwards *Daily Mail*, 7 February 2003)

Sport is a social context in which commentators can use and mix metaphors to an unprecedented degree. In the first noun phrase, the source may well be Shakespeare's *Richard III*, but it is worth noting that for many English people of a certain age it might recall the winter of 1978–1979, when Britain was going through a period of major industrial unrest, and which became known, through the media, as 'the winter of discontent'. (The Shakespearian context actually reads 'Now is the winter of *our* discontent'.)

Anfield is, as every British soccer fan knows, Liverpool Football Club's home base. The phrase *Anfield winter of discontent* has been placed in theme position in the headline: theme is what the reader sees first in a clause or sentence and so can be of strategic significance for a writer wishing to put forward a particular point of view. The metaphor has extra potency because, in addition to targeting the *discontent* of the Liverpool supporters, it was literally winter at the time the article appeared. Liverpool had not been playing well and this provides the second metaphor of the headline with all its connotation of animal or mob savagery. Think of a dog 'turning on' its owner or a mob 'turning on' a political leader. The headline is followed by a description of Liverpool Football Club's poor performance at a crucial stage of the British soccer season and the subsequent dissatisfaction of their supporters. The writer describes how the then Liverpool manager ('the boss'), Gerard Houllier, was being severely criticized by many of the club's supporters ('the fans').

In another, longer article from the same paper we have the headline:

OWEN SHOULDN'T BE **THE SCAPEGOAT**

(Compare the use of the same metaphor in *The Independent*'s account of the resignation of CIA director George Tenet. Here, we have further evidence of items being used in different contexts as part of the discourse of journalism, as in the case of *wound* earlier.)

In the context in which the metaphor is used here, the writer takes a sympathetic view of Michael Owen, one of the top players at Liverpool at that time. Owen had been criticized by some fans and journalists for Liverpool's relatively poor performances. The *Daily Mail* is quite explicit in its alternative view. Towards the end of the article, John Giles, the writer, sums up his opinions on Owen as a footballer. Giles's point is that Michael Owen has not been allowed to realize his potential as a player, but that this is not entirely his fault:

> The starting point is to turn Owen into **a genuine asset** rather than **a handy scapegoat**. He is a player **to be nourished** and **served** – not **fed scraps** in the desperate hope that he will turn **them** ['the scraps'] into **a banquet**.

In the highlighted items in the first sentence, we have a clear indication of Giles's stance as regards Michael Owen. There is the repetition of the headline *scapegoat* (taking the blame for the whole team) and the use of *asset*. An *asset* is someone or something of value and in the plural has strong connotations of property and possessions against which one's liabilities may be offset. Michael Owen is, of course, a person of value in terms of his sporting skills, but he was also one of Liverpool's *assets* in terms of money. They bought him, and eventually sold him on to Real Madrid. At one level, then, there is the concept of the player as a valuable investment and possession.

The concept of food and eating is here used to boost the writer's belief that Owen's team mates were not contributing as they should. Giles makes it clear that, from his point of view, the responsibility is Gerard Houllier's to ensure that other team members support Owen effectively on the football field. They should not be simply *feeding him scraps*. In making his point, in what is quite a long article, Giles also employs the concept of Houllier as a piano player:

> He reminds me of **a desperate pianist in pursuit of a lost chord**.

And two columns further on:

> Recovery of the **lost chord** seems as remote as ever

One of the most common of metaphorical usages in sport has to do with the concept of war, where WAR is the source for the target SPORT. Kövecses (2002: 75) makes the point that 'Many prototypical sports such as soccer, rugby, American football, wrestling, boxing, evolved from war and fighting.' The SPORT IS WAR metaphor can be seen exemplified in the two headlines below:

Big guns go into battle over Keane

> (Richard Tanner and Harry Harris *Daily Express*, 15 October 2002)

Wayne's Waterloo

> (Will Buckley *The Observer*, 2 February 2003)

The first headline refers to a controversy which involved the Manchester United and Irish international player Roy Keane. The second concerns the (then) Everton player, Wayne Rooney.

Similarly, from cricket:

Caddick digs in after the wipe-out of Nasser & Co

> **The tourists struggled** to 221 against a **sub-strength** Western Australia side . . .
>
> Hussein's team . . . were only **saved from** further embarrassment by **a rearguard action led by Andy Caddick**.

> (Graham Otway *Daily Mail*, 25 October 2002)

You might now like to unpack the war metaphors above.

METAPHOR AND ADVERTISING

Kövecses makes the point that:

> Part of the selling power of an advertisement depends on how well-chosen the conceptual metaphor is that the picture and/or the words used in the advertisement attempt to evoke in people. An appropriately selected metaphor may work wonders in promoting the sale of an item.

> (Kövecses 2002: 59)

For example, in an advertisement for Douwe Egbert's coffee, there is a picture of two packets of the coffee and a partially obscured cafetière and coffee cup. There follows a question with the answer supplied:

Love coffee?
Prepare to be smitten

(The Observer (Food Monthly), June 2003)

There is an element of personification here and we have seen something of this phenomenon already in this book. Personification is not new in the language of advertising. Consider this extract from a 1980s advertisement for a Ford Capri car:

It has **a low, wide stance**
It has **a muscular engine**
It is **a charismatic coupe**
Which has **always promised performance**

The car is presented in sexual terms; the sexuality, in fact, of the male. This is achieved by ascribing human, male attributes to the pronoun *it*. The coffee advertisement is, perhaps, less overtly sexual but the sexual element is there, nonetheless.

Make it a *real* **good time**. [Their italics]

Another advertisement, for washing machine detergent, comes from the women's magazine *Red* and also involves personification as one of its selling strategies. The advertisement opens with a question under a picture of a washing machine with a large duvet spilling out of it:

What do you **feed a machine** with **an appetite this big**?

(Red, March 2003)

The body copy reads as follows:

You've put a bigger load in the washing machine. There was even room for your duvet. That's the Indesit WAX 120 for you. But how do you get it all clean? Easy. Instead of one, just pop a couple of **Ariel Liquitabs** in the drum. Simple to use and highly concentrated, **Ariel Liquitabs tackle stains with so much energy they clean even the largest load**. No wonder Indesit **recommend** them.

The advertisement concludes with a slogan under a small picture of the detergent:

That's another load off your mind.

The slogan, of course, plays on the pun of *load*: that is, the literal *load*, 'something heavy', as in *a load of washing*, and the metaphorical *load*, indicating worry or anxiety. The machine is represented as having *appetite*: it is personified (or 'animalified'!). So are the two tablets of detergent. The consumer has to put them in the washing machine but the real work is done by the *Ariel Liquitabs*:

They can tackle
They have energy
They can clean

In other words, *they* (the Liquitabs) are seen as having agency. In addition, the use of punning helps to highlight the personification of the detergent as a 'friend' who can *take another load off your mind*. As Kövecses points out:

washing powders are frequently presented as good friends; this is based on the metaphor ITEMS TO SELL ARE PEOPLE, which is a kind of personification. A WASHING POWDER IS A FRIEND metaphor evokes in people the same attitudes and feelings that they have in connection with their good friends.

(Kövecses 2002: 59)

Indesit, of course, is also a good friend, as 'they' *recommend* Ariel Liquitabs. The young, professional female reader *doesn't have to do the washing herself* as the onerous nature of the task *is undertaken by her friends*. We have to say, however, we were unable to find any WASHING POWDER AS FRIENDS metaphors in similar, male magazines. In fact, we were unable to find any advertisements for washing powders whatsoever: is this ideology again?

Another example from *Red* also employs personification. Called *The Dream Team*, the advertisement features two Clinique products for women:

These **insomniacs work all night to defuse** the aging effects of time, stress, environment. **New Repairwear Intensive Night Cream helps block and mend** the look of lines and wrinkles. If skin's in need of more intensive

> treatment, add new **Repairwear Extra Help Serum to elevate the potential for repairing** skin's appearance. Clinique. Allergy Tested. 100% Fragrance Free.

Note how the two versions of the product, *Clinique Repairwear Intensive Night Cream* and *Clinique Repairwear Extra Help Serum*, are given human agency: personification again! The products are:

insomniacs who can work all night.

Specifically:

Insomniac 1 helps block and mend

while those who require further treatment can rely on:

Insomniac 2 to elevate the potential for repairing skin's appearance.

Note also the use of the scientific item *serum* as a metaphor. Many advertisements employ pseudo scientific or technical language in the belief that this will help boost sales because it implies a professional expertise.

METAPHOR AND MONEY

Money involves all of us: the earning of it, the spending of it, how to get more, insufficient funds, and so on. For example, consider the metaphor below, which is reworked three times, but in different sections of the British broadsheet Sunday newspaper, *The Observer*. First, as a headline:

Hands down
You can always win if you play your cards right

(The Observer (Cash), 2 February 2003)

This appeared as a headline on the front cover of the *Observer* supplement *Cash*. It was strongly supported by a non-verbal metaphor, a full-length colour illustration of a card game with two pairs of hands. One pair was foregrounded so that the *Observer* reader could be said to be 'sitting in the player's place'. The cards being held were credit cards and on the centre of the table were some gambling chips.

On page 2 we have an article on credit card use (and abuse) and which is continued through to page 4. The headline for the article is:

Card sharps beat the system

A further headline on page 3 extends the gambling metaphor to

Tips for card sharps

And it extends even more, from the tabloid format *Cash*, to the Observer's broadsheet *Business and Media* supplement of the same day with, in the top right-hand corner of page 1, a reduced copy of *Cash's* cover illustration and the caption:

Great deal: Make your cards come up trumps

The article referred to focused on one man's ability to keep on top of credit card debt by the astute use of the balance transfer deals which many of the credit card companies offer at low interest rates or, indeed, 0 per cent for a limited period.

A strategy now used by banks is to see their customers as consumers buying actual merchandise. This occurs to the extent that it can be found in spoken situations as in face-to-face interaction with bank staff, as well as in the written mode. For example, compare the following. First, from the Lloyds/TSB Platinum Account Pack, exemplifying the concept MONEY IS A PRODUCT:

Best rates of interest offered by Lloyds/TSB on **this type of product**

and second:

'We value your custom highly . . . we know that you have availed yourselves of a number of **our products**'.
(Personal conversation with Bank Manager, November 2002)

What is interesting here is the fact that the *product* referred to in the first of these extracts concerns overdraft facilities, while the second is referring to a discussion about an application for a bank loan. In neither case is the text referring to something physical, produced by manufacture.

Another metaphorical expression in financial discourse is based on the concept of being *locked in*. This can concern a mortgage, as in this first example from a Cheltenham and Gloucester Building Society advertisement:

> No **lock-in** period

or in the BBC's reporting on the Bank of England's decision to cut interest rates:

> these interest rates have been **locked in**
>
> (BBC Radio 4, PM at 5pm, 6 February 2003)

or in a variation of *lock in* used by the Abbey National Building Society, also in an advertisement:

> Great rates on Mortgages . . . no extended **tie ins**.

Another source exploited in money metaphor involves the concept of FIRE or HEAT. Heat, of course, signifies intensity. Kövecses (2002: 112–117) discusses the concepts of FIRE and HEAT and their association with emotions such as ANGER and LOVE: see also our discussions in earlier chapters. In the financial world, decisions by governments and big business can create a situation that affects virtually everyone. The cause of this situation is the cause of the *heat* or *fire* (2002: 115). Thus, from the same BBC current affairs programme cited above we have the following:

> Do you think this could **re-ignite** the housing market? . . . There's been a **blaze** there anyway.

So, the interviewee is being asked, 'will the cut in interest rates cause a situation which in turn will cause *fire (re-ignition)*?' But we are told a little later in the interview that the situation of house prices has already caused *fire (a blaze)*.

On the same topic, Alex Brummer of the *Daily Mail* also uses, amongst other metaphors, the concept of HEAT:

> if the choice is a temporary reduction in savings' rates versus a Japanese or a German-style **meltdown**, then a **sacrifice** on rates must be more **palatable**.
> (*Daily Mail*, 7 February 2003)

As well as *meltdown*, note the contrast between the concept of giving something up (*sacrifice*: remember this item in the reporting of the news), that is the lowering of interest rates which adversely affects savers, and that of something appetizing (*palatable*) and therefore more acceptable, from the point of view of maintaining financial stability.

In referring to house prices, Brummer comments that in many parts of Britain house prices are going up. This is not true of:

overheated London and the South-East.

Also in Brummer's article, we can see the GOOD IS UP, BAD IS DOWN contrast, as in

> It is not often during the past 15 months of interest rates that industrialists have had the opportunity to **throw their hats in the air**.

and quoting Digby Jones of the Confederation of British Industry:

'**This should put some wind under the wings of industry**'

Finally, just prior to the war with Iraq:

> it is too much to expect that a quarter point cut will be enough **to lift the market out of the doldrums**.

Now, interpret the following four money metaphors in terms of topic, vehicle, and grounds:

a German style meltdown

overheated London and the South East

to throw their hats in the air

to lift the market out of the doldrums

GRAMMATICAL METAPHOR

So far in this book, we have concentrated on examples of lexical metaphor. There is, however, a textual phenomenon, known as **grammatical metaphor**. In grammatical metaphor or nominalization (see Halliday 1994: 342–367) actions, which would usually be described by a sentence such as *we study economics*, are presented in a noun phrase such as *the study of economics*. At its most simple, activities or processes, which would naturally be expressed by verbs, become *things*. The verbs have been changed into nouns: they have become nominalized. English is a language in which it is possible to use nominalization to quite a large extent, especially in the written form and the more formal spoken varieties. We have choices in English as to how we want to present situations and events to others. There will be a typical or 'congruent' way, as in *we study economics*, or there is the metaphorical way. Ideologically, nominalization allows the writer or speaker to avoid mentioning the agent or 'doer' of the action. In our basic example above, we avoided mentioning the *we* when we reformulated *we study economics* as *the study of economics*.

The Australian linguist Jim Martin (1985: 43) has demonstrated how grammatical metaphor can be exploited in texts to avoid, or at least to disguise, situations that might be evaluated as unpleasant in some way. In exemplification, Martin cites two texts that have a common theme. One argues that the culling of kangaroos is brutal and should be stopped. The other is a 'pro culling' text. The latter puts forward the point of view that culling, in this case of baby seals, is a sensible, scientific business. Both texts have distinctive styles in arguing their cases. The 'kangaroo' text is much more emotive and draws attention to the active processes involved in the culling and those who are the agents of those processes. It uses more congruent forms in its argument. The seal text, on the other hand, draws attention away from these unpleasant activities. One device used by the seal killing lobby is nominalization. The use of this grammatical metaphor, as Martin points out, disguises the highly active and brutal nature of the processes. Thus, instead of *the hunters clubbed the baby seals to death* we have:

the seal hunt

or

the sealing operation

or, even more ideologically sited,

the white coat harvest

So, in the three extracts above, the agents (the 'cullers'/killers) are not mentioned and what they do (club baby seals to death) is 'hidden' by careful language selection.

In the completely different area of Forensic Stylistics, Malcolm Coulthard's work demonstrates how disputed sentences in statements made to the police can show the feature of nominalization. He cites examples of 'the representation of *processes*, which are typically reported by verbs in spoken English as *products*, which are encoded as nominal(ization)s' (his italics) (1995: 241): in other words, features which are more typical of written discourse. Coulthard gives, in exemplification, the first sentence of a statement attributed to a defendant but which the defendant claimed was only partly an authentic record:

> I wish to make a further statement explaining my complete involvement in the hijacking of the Ford Escort van from John Smith on Tuesday 28 March 1981 on behalf of the A.B.C. which was later used in the murder of three person [*sic*] in Avon that night.
>
> (Coulthard 1995: 240–241)

The defendant claimed that much of his statement had been invented by police officers. Coulthard takes from the sentence above four grammatical metaphors:

make **a statement**

complete involvement

the hijacking

the murder

As Coulthard points out, 'It was possible to argue that this was not as the police claimed a verbatim record of what the accused had said.' In fact, under cross-examination, the police officer 'conceded that the statement may not after all have been verbatim'. He continued to maintain, however, that the defendant had spoken all the words but 'perhaps not in that order'. See Coulthard (1995: 241–242) for further discussion.

In sum, lexical metaphors can provide creativity in language, in the special way in which they convey meaning. Furthermore, they can help in vigorously putting forward a point of view. If lexical metaphors can present one kind of truth as opposed to another, then, equally, grammatical metaphor can be organized to obscure the truth or 'the facts', or to present activities in a more favourable light.

SUMMARY

In this chapter, we have looked at the relationship between metaphor and society, and at how metaphor can be used by writers and speakers to support beliefs or points of view.

We saw how, in political biography, metaphor was used stylistically as part of a non-fiction narrative describing the relationship between two very senior British politicians. In the media, we focused on the report of the resignation of a leading British politician and of some of the participants in that event. We also discussed metaphor in sports reporting and demonstrated that metaphor is not necessarily context-specific and that some lexical items can be categorized as part of the discourse of journalism. In our case, items like *wound*, *scapegoat*, and *sacrifice* were used in both news and sports reporting.

In advertising, we considered metaphor being employed persuasively to sell things. We should also bear in mind that the pictures or 'images' of advertisements can be seen as metaphors or the non-verbal or visual realization of metaphor. Non-verbal metaphor will be our focus in Chapter 9.

In the context of money, we saw how banks and other institutions view money as a product to be purchased by consumers. We looked at the concepts of HEAT and FIRE and their realization in money metaphors, and we also took note of examples of up/down positive/negative polarity.

Finally, we showed how two linguists have investigated grammatical metaphor, and how this phenomenon can be used to obscure unpleasantness or to be evasive with the truth.

These are not the only contexts in which language generally, and metaphor specifically, evaluates or puts forward a point of view. In religious discourse, for example, metaphor can play a major role. Think, for instance, of the concept, THE CHURCH IS A FAMILY, and expressions such as 'mother church' and 'daughter church'. There is also the concept of RELIGION IS A GROWING THING. In the Christian religion, there are hymns which use the items, 'root', 'branch', and 'stem', and such imagery is also to be found in the Bible, particularly in the Old Testament. Religion also, as we will see in Chapter 9, effectively employs non-verbal metaphor.

FURTHER READING

Bolinger, D. (1980) *Language – the Loaded Weapon*, London: Longman. (General discussion of ideological aspects of vocabulary.)

Cameron, L. (2003) *Metaphor in Educational Discourse*, London and New York: Continuum. (Investigates metaphorical language in the classroom and educational contexts.)

Charteris-Black, J. (2004) *Politicians and Rhetoric: the Persuasive Power of Metaphor*, Basingstoke: Palgrave. (Investigates the use of metaphor in politics.)

Cook, G. (1992) *The Discourse of Advertising*, London: Routledge.

Fairclough, N. (1989) *Language and Power*, London: Longman. (Discussion of ideology in language.)

Goatly, A. (1997) *The Language of Metaphors*, London: Routledge. (Chapter 10.)

Kövecses, Z. (2002) *Metaphor: a Practical Introduction*, Oxford: Oxford University Press. (Chapters 1 and 2.)

Lakoff, G. and Johnson, M. (1980; new edn 2003) *Metaphors we Live by*, Chicago: University of Chicago Press. (Discussion of how metaphor is used ideologically in, for example, Chapters 21–23.)

Martin, J.R. (1985) *Factual Writing: Exploring and Challenging Social Reality*, Victoria, Australia: Deakin University Press; republished (1989) Oxford: Oxford University Press. (Discussion of grammatical metaphor.)

Montgomery, M. (1995) *An Introduction to Language and Society*, 2nd edn, London: Routledge. (Chapters 5 and 6 for useful discussion of language and the context of situation.)

Vestergaard, T. and Schrøder, K. (1985) *The Language of Advertising*, Oxford: Blackwell.

8

LITERARY METAPHOR

Most of us probably made our first conscious acquaintance with metaphorical language in the study of literary texts: novels, drama, poetry, and so on. Language is 'made strange' in some way or **foregrounded**, so that it is different from other everyday usages although, as Kövecses (2002: 44) points out, creative writers very often base their work on the same conceptual metaphors that we all use in day-to-day existence. Notwithstanding this fact, creative metaphor is an essential literary ingredient. In Chapter 1, we pointed out that the term **metaphor** applies to several different linguistic phenomena, and we looked at some of the different types of non-literal language of which metaphor is the best-known form. We will now consider the most important of these which constitute the creative devices available to writers of literary text. As we do so, it is useful to remember that metaphorical language is, to varying degrees, ambiguous, and we will look at ambiguity itself later in this chapter.

READING BETWEEN THE LINES

As we have seen throughout this book, our understanding of metaphorical language depends not only on our linguistic competence but our cultural sensitivity, and our knowledge of more than just the surface structure of the words on the page. It is all very well for Humpty Dumpty to claim that when he uses a word, 'it means just what I choose it to mean – neither more nor less' (see Carroll *Through the Looking Glass* 1871/1970: 269), but *meaning* must have some form of general agreement among language users if meaningful communication is to take place. Nowhere is this truer than in the decoding of literary texts. Consider the short extract below from Jane Austen:

> It is a truth universally acknowledged, that a single man in possession of a good fortune, must be in want of a wife.

This is one of the most famous examples of irony in English literature and is the opening sentence from *Pride and Prejudice* (1813). **Irony** is a device used by many writers, and presents the reader with a situation where the author intends the meaning of his or her words to be interpreted differently and usually in a way opposite to their literal meaning. In other words, the surface meanings are opposed to the meanings that underlie the text.

The irony in the example lies in the fact that this sentence sets the scene for the novel and its topic of marriage. The truth of the statement is far from *universal*, but the mothers of unmarried young daughters take the statement as a fact: that is, the appearance of the rich young man causes them to behave accordingly in the pursuance of obtaining husbands for their daughters.

It is in the literary domain that we can see especially how writers exploit symbolism and imagery, as well as devices such as puns and irony. For example, consider the following extract from *Richard III* (Act I scene 1), already mentioned in Chapter 7:

> Now is the winter of our discontent
> Made glorious summer by this sun of York.

In another example, from an untitled poem by Auden, the intensity of death or loss is captured as follows:

> He was my North, my South, my East and West,
> My working week and my Sunday rest,
> My noon, my midnight, my talk, my song . . .
>
> (Auden 1966: 92)

What Shakespeare and Auden write is literally untrue, but nonetheless both extracts have validity and reality in terms of metaphorical and emotional meaning. Both examples illustrate the fact that metaphors are literally untrue, at least at some level. We have already made this point more than once, but it is worth reiterating in the context of this chapter.

TROPES AND SCHEMES

We have already given a general definition of metaphorical language and we now offer a more precise consideration of this term in relation to its use in literary texts. To repeat, metaphorical language means a departure from what language users perceive as the standard norm in terms of the meaning of words. As such, it is part of **figurative language**, which can also mean a departure from standard word order. In literary theory, when rhetoricians have talked of figurative language they have often attempted to distinguish between **tropes**, or changes or conversions in meaning, and **schemes** or **figures** (figures of speech or rhetorical figures), where word order provides the special effects. Shakespeare, Auden, and Austen provided us with examples of trope. Irony is a trope, as are simile, metonymy, symbolism, personification, and allegory. Metaphor itself is a major trope.

Schemes are not the focus of this chapter but it is important to mention them, albeit briefly, as, for many scholars, the differentiation between tropes and schemes is not nowadays considered to be so clear-cut. The first stanza from one of Gerard Manley Hopkins's most famous poems provides an example of a scheme: in this particular instance, **alliteration** which is the repetition of initial consonants (many of these sounds also occur internally in the words):

God's **G**randeur

The **w**orld is charged **w**ith the **g**randeur of **G**od.
It will **f**lame out, like **sh**ining **f**rom **sh**ook **f**oil;
It **g**athers to a **g**reatness, like the ooze of oil
Crushed. Why do men then **n**ow **n**ot **r**eck his **r**od?

Other examples of schemes are **assonance** or the repetition of identical vowel sounds as in:

> Thou still unravished bride of quietness!
> Thou foster-child of Silence and slow Time . . .

from Keats's 'Ode on a Grecian Urn'. This extract also provides an example of **apostrophe**. This involves the addressing of someone imaginary or absent or even dead, or something that cannot actually listen or is an abstraction. For example, consider these opening lines of Yeats's 'Reconciliation':

> Some may have blamed **you** that **you** took away
> The verses that could move them on the day
> When, the ears being deafened, the sight of the eyes blind
> With lightning, **you** went from me, and I could find
> Nothing to make a song about but kings,
> Helmets, and swords, and half-forgotten things
> That were like memories of **you** –
>
> (Yeats 1950: 102)

The addressee is the absent Maud Gonne. She was the love of Yeats's life but did not return that love. Yeats received the news of Maud Gonne's marriage to John MacBride just before he was to give a lecture. Yeats claimed to have no recall of what he said in that lecture. The important point is that there are different types of way in which figurative language can foreground the language of literary text.

METONYMY IN LITERATURE

Metonymy is, of course, a major trope: as we saw in Chapters 1 and 4, metonymy involves applying the literal term for one thing to another, where one is part of the other, or where there is a close association between them, such as *the Crown* for the monarchy. The distinguished linguist Roman Jakobson (1960) differentiated between metaphor and metonymy in stating that metaphor is a relationship between two different entities based on similarity, whereas metonymy is a contiguous relationship. In other words, metonymy exploits one or more features of the literal meaning, but part of the literal meaning remains, as in the *Crown/monarchy* example. The critic and novelist David Lodge also takes up this distinction in his book *The Modes of Modern Writing* (1977). Consider the use of metonymy in this well-known example from James Shirley's 'The Glories of Our Blood and State' (*c.* 1633):

> Sceptre and Crown
> Must tumble down,
> And in the dust be equal made
> With the poor crooked scythe and spade.

What are the metonyms here and what do they stand for?

A good example from a literary narrative comes from Dickens. In *Little Dorrit*, he made use of body parts to represent one of his characters, Mrs Merdle, when he refers to her as *the bosom*:

> **The bosom** moving in Society with the jewels displayed upon it, attracted general admiration.
>
> (Dickens 1857: Chapter 21)

> Mrs Merdle's first husband had been a colonel, under whose auspices **the bosom** had entered into competition with the snows of North America, and had come off at little disadvantage in point of whiteness, and at none in point of coldness.
>
> (Dickens 1857: Chapter 21)

Is there any hint of irony in the above extracts?

For some, these Mrs Merdle examples would be classified as synecdoche. However, as we pointed out in Chapter 4, distinguishing between metonymy and synecdoche can be problematic, and so we will continue to refer to both phenomena as metonymy.

PERSONIFICATION AS METAPHOR

With the major tropes of metaphor and metonymy we can also include **personification** which, as we noted in Chapter 1, can be seen in terms of metaphorical transfer and anthropomorphism. Personification is, then, the attribution of human properties to inanimate objects. Compare the device in myths and fairy stories where people turn into stones, trees walk, rivers speak, and so on. For example, in Oscar Wilde's famous fairy story, *The Happy Prince* (1888):

> Wherever he went the Sparrows chirruped, and **said to each other**, 'what a distinguished stranger!'

the sparrows are *talking* about the Swallow, a major character in the narrative, who can also talk: 'I am waited for in Egypt', he says, referring to his fellow swallows who have migrated for the winter. The other major character is, of course, the Prince himself. He is a statue, he is inanimate, but, like the Swallow, he can talk:

'Dear little Swallow,' **said the Prince**, 'you **tell me** of marvellous things, but more marvellous than anything is the suffering of men and of women. There is no Mystery so great as Misery. Fly over my city, little Swallow, and **tell me** what you see there.'

Now consider this extract from Tolkien's *The Two Towers* and explain the metaphorical significance of the highlighted elements:

Treebeard strode up the slope, hardly slackening his pace. Suddenly before them the hobbits saw a wide opening. **Two great trees stood there, one on either side, like living gate posts**; but there was no gate save their crossing and interwoven boughs. As the old Ent approached **the trees lifted up their branches and all their leaves quivered and rustled**.

(Tolkien 1954/1993: 85)

Personification has always been widely used as a literary device especially in lyric poetry. Wordsworth's personified daffodils below demonstrate what is probably one of the best-known, to the point of cliché, examples of this type of metaphor:

Ten thousand saw I at a glance
Tossing their heads in sprightly dance

Apostrophe (see above) can also be associated with personification by implication, in that where an abstract or inanimate entity is addressed by a writer the reader may assume that it is endowed with human life. Keats does this in his 'Ode on a Grecian Urn' referred to earlier, as does Wilfred Owen in his poem 'Elegy in April and September', where he also addresses daffodils:

Be still, daffodil!
And **wave me** not so bravely.

Your gay gold lily daunts me and deceives,
Who follow gleams more golden and more slim.

(Owen 1963: 142)

METAPHOR, AMBIGUITY, AND LITERATURE

We pointed out earlier that ambiguity is associated with metaphorical language, as when Mercutio says, after being fatally wounded:

Ask for me tomorrow, and you shall find me a **grave** man

(*Romeo and Juliet*, Act 3 scene 1)

Mercutio's utterance is illustrative of one of the many creative devices that constitute metaphorical language in literary texts. Many of the terms are highly specialist, but some of the more commonly known would include Mercutio's utterance, which we would recognize as an example of **pun**. Shakespeare made much use of punning both for comic and serious effect. In punning, the writer makes a play on words where the sound is identical or very similar but the meaning is different. Lewis Carroll placed great emphasis on this type of ambiguity, as the following extracts demonstrate. Note how the ambiguity exists in the speech of the characters, where one word can stand for something quite different:

'Mine is a long and sad **tale**!' said the Mouse . . .
    'It *is* a long **tail**, certainly,' said Alice, looking down with wonder at the Mouse's tail; 'but why do you call it sad?'

(Carroll 1865/1970: 50)

'That's the reason they're called **lessons**', the Gryphon remarked: 'because they **lessen** from day to day.'

(Carroll 1865/1970: 130)

These two extracts come from *Alice's Adventures in Wonderland*. The third comes from *Through the Looking Glass*:

'How is bread made?'
    'I know *that*!' Alice cried eagerly. 'You take some flour – '
    'Where do you pick the flower?' the White Queen asked. 'In a garden or in the hedges?'

> 'Well, it isn't *picked* at all,' Alice explained: 'it's *ground* – '
> 'How many acres of ground?'
>
> (Carroll 1871/1970: 322)

In this extract, the ambiguity between *flour/flower* and the two meanings of *ground* causes a conversation to lose direction.

Carroll had a predilection for punning, which not only reflected his preoccupation with the nature of language but also served other purposes. Carroll used his 'Alice' narratives to tilt at some Victorian windmills (note our use of metaphorical language!). For example, the following is taken from the episode in Chapter 2 of *Alice's Adventures in Wonderland*, where Alice and the Mouse are immersed in the Pool of Tears. Here, Carroll plays on the meanings of *dry* as in 'not wet' and 'uninterestingly expressed' to reinforce his criticism of Victorian educational practices:

> The first question of course was, how to get **dry** again: they had a consultation about this . . .
>
> At last the Mouse, who seemed to be a person of some authority among them, called out, 'Sit down all of you and listen to me! *I'll* soon make you **dry** enough!' . . .
>
> 'Ahem!' said the Mouse with an important air. 'Are you all ready? This is the **driest** thing I know. Silence all round, if you please! "William the Conqueror, whose cause was favoured by the pope, was soon submitted to by the English, who wanted leaders, and had been of late much accustomed to usurpation and protest. Edwin and Morcar, the earls of Mercia and Northumbria – "'
>
> (Carroll 1871/1970: 45–46)

And so it goes on and on and on. The Mouse is attempting to *dry off* the gathered assembly by reciting a passage from a history book which had actually been used by the Liddell children (see Gardner 1970: 46, note 1): Alice Liddell was the daughter of the Dean of Oxford, and the model for Alice in both *Alice's Adventures in Wonderland* and *Through the Looking Glass*. However, the *dry* educational oration does not have the desired effects in the 'real' world in either of its senses. Alice complains, *it doesn't seem to dry me at all* (1865/1970: 47), and the sheer monotony of the Mouse's oration reflects Carroll's views on Victorian education.

Lewis Carroll also exploited multiple meaning with his **portmanteau** words in *Through the Looking Glass*:

> 'Twas **brillig** and the **slithy** toves
> Did gyre and gimble in the wabe:
> All mimsy were the borogoves,
> And the mome raths outgrabe.
> > (Carroll 1871/1970: 191)

It is Humpty Dumpty who tries to interpret the poem for Alice:

> ' "*Brillig*" means four o'clock in the afternoon – the time when you begin *broiling* things for dinner.'
>
> 'That'll do very well,' said Alice: 'and "*slithy*"?'
>
> 'Well, "*slithy*" means "lithe and slimy" . . . You see it's like a portmanteau – there are two meanings packed up into one word.'
> > (Carroll 1871/1970: 270–271)

James Joyce, of course, developed Carroll's technique to perfection in *Finnegans Wake*, which, like *Alice's Adventures in Wonderland*, is a dream experience. For example, Joyce refers to girls who are, 'yung and easily freudened' (1939/1964: 115): here *young* and *Jung* are blended, as are *frightened* and *Freud*.

SYMBOLISM AND ALLEGORY

We have already said in this book that metaphor is a form of symbol, and certainly all the uses of metaphorical language which we have talked about in this chapter can be seen as symbols. **Symbolism** itself, of course, may play an important role in literature. We commented in Chapter 1 on how symbols can be public in our culture, and also on how they exist in other media. In literature, the symbols employed by writers can sometimes be private or personal, and this can pose problems for the reader in the interpretation of what the writer actually means. Coleridge's 'Rime of the Ancient Mariner' represents a major symbolic work, and in the early decades of the twentieth century, the work of Yeats employed a range of symbols, including the tower and the phases of the moon, which embody the poet's personal philosophy.

Children's writers have often used symbols in their narratives. One of the most well-known is the symbol of the kitchen where it stands for safety and comradeship. This can be seen in the following description of Badger's kitchen in Kenneth Grahame's *The Wind in the Willows*: objects are here presented as anthropomorphic.

> The ruddy brick floor smiled up at the smoky ceiling; the oaken settles, shiny with long wear, exchanged cheerful glances with each other; plates on the dresser grinned at pots on the shelf, and the merry firelight flickered and played over everything without distinction.
>
> (Grahame 1908/1951: 44)

Interestingly, the kitchen symbol can also be used in the opposite way, as Carpenter (1985: 163) points out, when he shows the kitchen symbolizing moral decay in this extract from George MacDonald's *The Princess and Curdie*:

> Everywhere was filth and disorder. Mangy turnspit dogs were lying about, and grey rats were gnawing at refuse in the sinks ... [Curdie] longed for one glimpse of his mother's poor little kitchen, so clean and bright and airy.
>
> (MacDonald 1883/1990: 317)

Gardens too can be symbolic, of course, if we think of Frances Hodgson Burnett's *The Secret Garden*, or Philippa Pearce's *Tom's Midnight Garden*, and many other pieces of literature, including medieval literature.

Allegory itself represents a metaphorical representation, and we commented in Chapter 1 on the moral significance of allegorical meaning. For example, John Bunyan's *The Pilgrim's Progress* is a moral and religious allegory. Other writers such as Jonathan Swift use allegory to satirize, as does George Orwell, in whose work the hidden meanings are political and social rather than moral or religious. C.S. Lewis uses allegory in his re-telling of the Christian story for children. *The Lion, the Witch and the Wardrobe*, for example, depends very much on the narrative of Christ's passion and the Resurrection:

> 'Oh, it's *too* bad' sobbed Lucy, 'they might have left the body alone.'
>
> 'Who's done it?' cried Susan. 'What does it mean? Is it magic?'
>
> 'Yes!' said a great voice behind their backs. 'It is more magic.' They looked round. There, shining in the sunrise, larger than they had seen him before, shaking his mane (for it had apparently grown again) stood Aslan himself.
>
> 'Oh, Aslan!' cried both the children, staring up at him, almost as much frightened as they were glad.

'Aren't you dead then, dear Aslan?' said Lucy.
'Not now,' said Aslan.

(Lewis 1950/1988: 147)

Whole narratives, then, can be seen as structured around metaphors. In fact, as Kövecses (2002: 65) points out, complete sub-genres of literature can be seen in terms of the LIFE IS A JOURNEY metaphor. He cites Bunyan's *Pilgrim's Progress* as a good example from one such sub-genre: compare also the classical epics the *Odyssey* and the *Aeneid*, which relate the adventures of a returning warrior, or medieval stories of quests and pilgrimages, such as in Arthurian literature or Chaucer's *The Canterbury Tales*. In children's literature, in the classical adventure stories of the nineteenth and early twentieth centuries, the narratives usually follow the path of an adolescent British male hero on an imperial journey to Africa or India. Here, the LIFE IS A JOURNEY metaphor is not concerned with the complete life of the hero. Rather, it is that part of his life in which he has to prove himself by being exposed to various dangers and temptations. These he ultimately overcomes, and he returns home an older and wiser man: his physical journey is matched by the journey of his developing maturity as he 'travels' into full manhood.

WRITERS, READERS, AND METAPHOR

Many writers construct propositions through figurative or metaphorical language, and we readers have to make our minds up as to the meaning being conveyed to us. In so doing, writers are also establishing their relationship with their readers. The important point about metaphor in literature is that it can make you, the reader, think. What exactly is the writer getting at? Remember, all writers have an image of the reader in mind when they construct their narrative, and we can refer to this image as the implied reader. Equally, we as readers have an image of the type of person the author is as we deconstruct the text. The concepts of implied author and of implied reader are useful precisely because they help us understand the author's relationship with the reader. One of the ways in which we can come to grips with this relationship is by developing our ability to recognize the devices of figurative language used in creating a text. In recognizing these devices, we become aware of their contribution to the construction of meaning in the text.

Let's consider the extracts below which come from the children's book *Carrie's War* by Nina Bawden:

> But Miss Evans looked nice; a little like **a red squirrel** Carrie had once seen, **peering round a tree in a park**.
>
> (Bawden 1973: 21)

> But Mr Evans didn't fly into the rage'she'd expected. He simply looked startled – **as if a worm had just lifted its head and answered him back**, Carrie thought.
>
> (Bawden 1973: 28)

> Her voice was pitched soft and low. **Her spell-binding voice**, Carrie thought . . . She was holding a candle and **her eyes shone in its light** and **her gleaming hair fell like silk on her shoulders**. **A beautiful witch**, Carrie thought.
>
> (Bawden 1973: 65)

> She looked at Mrs Gotobed's **claw-like, ringed fingers** holding her delicate cup and thought of Auntie Lou's little red hands that were always in water, washing dishes or scrubbing floors or peeling potatoes.
>
> (Bawden 1973: 71)

> **He was like a bear**, Carrie thought: **A friendly, silly, strong bear**.
>
> (Bawden 1973: 90)

The book tells the story of Carrie and her brother Nick who have been evacuated to a Welsh village during the Second World War. They are billeted with a shopkeeper, the bigoted and embittered Mr Evans and his browbeaten younger sister. Mr Evans is estranged from his elder sister, Mrs Gotobed, who lives in a nearby farmhouse, Druid's Bottom, with her housekeeper Hepzibah Green. The story revolves around the relationships that develop between Carrie and the other characters, and the contrast between the bleakness of the Evans household and the warmth and security of Hepzibah's kitchen at Druid's Bottom.

These extracts provide exemplification of another type of trope, **simile**, and it is this sort of use of figurative language that gives reinforcement to the writer's voice as she establishes her relationship with her child reader. Similes, of course, draw upon comparisons between two very different but explicit entities, and are signalled by items such as *like*, *as*, *compare*, or *resemble*, as we have already said.

The extracts demonstrate how Bawden uses figurative language in the development of her narrative. They come from episodes in the story where Carrie records her reaction to meeting a number of the adult characters either on first acquaintance or very early on in their relationship. Each of them is being evaluated and the author invites the reader to see things from Carrie's point of view. Nina Bawden, in a sense, gives us Carrie's 'eyes'. Carrie is apprehensive and a major strategy of conveying this state is the use of simile and animal imagery in four of the examples just cited. In each, a particular feature of the different characters is presented to the reader with either a positive or a negative sense. Consider the vehicles of the different similes above:

a red squirrel

a worm

claw-like ringed fingers

a friendly, silly, strong bear

This is exactly the sort of language a perceptive and sensitive child might use to record her impressions of the adults, often somewhat dysfunctional, who have replaced her family and her familiar world. It is through such strategies that Bawden conveys meaning to her child reader.

By contrast, consider Carrie's first impressions of Hepzibah as recorded in the third of the examples. First, we are told that: Hepzibah's voice is *soft and low*; it is a *spell-binding voice*; then *her eyes shone in its light*; and the simile *her gleaming hair fell like silk on her shoulders*; and finally (she is) *a beautiful witch*. There is no animal imagery here. Rather, we have the witch metaphor first introduced by *her spell-binding voice*: this is a benign (and beautiful) witch. We have further positive evaluation in *her eyes shone in its light*. It is almost as if Hepzibah's voice and eyes and hair are agents in their own right, that they can 'do things'. Note the contrast with Miss Evans's *little red hands*, which are also treated as agents, as they *were always in water, washing dishes or scrubbing floors or peeling potatoes*. Similarly, Mrs Gotobed's claw-like, ringed fingers are represented as *holding her delicate cup*. It does not matter that the human subjects control the hands. Like Hepzibah's voice, eyes, and hair, Miss Evans's and Mrs Gotobed's hands have agency. This kind of construction is rather like those where inanimate or abstract objects behave like people: that is, personification.

POT BOILERS, BODICE RIPPERS, AND WHODUNNITS

It is not just classical literature or 'serious' novels and poems that employ metaphorical language, but also popular fiction. In some genres this is usually to the extent that much of it results in cliché rather than in creative metaphor. In Chapter 3 we saw how Lakoff and Johnson identified metaphors for love and emotion and mental phenomena. Héloïse McGuinness (1998) constructed a corpus of such data from romantic popular fiction, and demonstrated how a part of the body or an emotion takes over as a focus for the action of the narrative as in

His eyes searched her angry green gaze . . .

or

Her green eyes flared . . .

Note again how parts of the body are ascribed agency. We give a few other examples from McGuinness's data below:

Her eyes stabbed him with daggers of pain . . .

She shot him with a chilling, black-eyed blast . . .

Her gaze slid over his shoulder and up . . .

She tore her gaze from him . . .

A suspicion wormed into Sarah's mind . . .

Suspicion and *gaze* are both personified, and Carter and Nash (1990: 107) make the point that sentences like those from McGuinness's data illustrate 'the myth of agency', as heroines are acted upon rather than acting for themselves. They also point to the 'metaphoric vitality' with which popular fiction writers pack their verbs, for example as in *stabbed* and *wormed* above, thus reinforcing the clichés that pervade so much of this kind of prose. In the second example, note the use of **nominalization** or **grammatical metaphor** (discussed in Chapter 7), where we have human agency and the metaphor contained in a verb + noun phrase, rather than in a structure such as 'her black eyes shot him with a chilling blast'.

Detective and mystery novels also use metaphorical devices in the structuring of their plots. Ian Rankin is one of Britain's top crime writers and presents his main character, Inspector Rebus, in a series of narratives conspicuous for their dry humour and sense of realism. The following extract from *Beggars Banquet* is typical of Rankin's style:

> Not that he would take one (a holiday): **the loneliness could be a cage as well as a release**. But he would never, he hoped, be **as caged as these people around him**. He looked for a Grebe Tours badge on any passing lapel or chest, but saw none. The Edinburgh Castle gatekeepers had been **eagle-eyed** alright, or one of them had ...
>
> (Rankin 2003: 195)

So, we have conceptual metaphors LONELINESS IS A CAGE, LONELINESS IS A RELEASE, and SOME PEOPLE ARE MORE IMPRISONED THAN OTHERS, and the metaphorical item *eagle-eyed*, referring to the ability to notice very small details. There are also metonymic uses in this extract: what are they, how and why are they metonyms?

Ruth Rendell is one of Britain's best-known mystery writers, and is regarded as an author who rises above the mundane or stereotypical detective narrative. Writing as Barbara Vine, she has produced a number of works renowned for depth of characterization and particular psychological shifts. These works are very different from the romantic novels discussed above. Rendell/Vine uses metaphorical language in deceptively simple ways and thus manages to create powerful atmospheric backdrops of scene to complement the flawed characters who inhabit her novels. Now, consider the following from Vine's *The Chimney Sweeper's Boy*, and unpack the metaphorical devices she uses:

> The Hampstead house was sold and they moved in December, the day after Sarah's fourth birthday. It was raining and the grey steely sea looked as if punctured all over by a million shining needles ... Next day the fog came. The house, the gardens, the dunes were swathed in it, muffled by it, and the sea was invisible. He reacted violently, saying he would never have bought the house if he'd known.
>
> (Vine 1998: 209)

A newer crime genre writer is Paul Bryers. Bryers, in fact, cannot be classified as simply 'a detective story writer'. His narrative style has strong overtones of black comedy, and one of the more interesting aspects of that style is the intertextual. Figurative language plays a key role in this, as the following extract from *The Used Women's Book Club* illustrates:

> Jo's marriage, like the title of the Used Women's Book Club, was a mistake. In her more confident, light-hearted moments she would describe it as a whim . . . a foolish but ultimately harmless fancy . . . At other times she **compared it to a disease**, one of those childhood **afflictions** that recur more **virulently** in later life, **like shingles**.
>
> 'I **caught it** from a book,' she would say, mysteriously, and change the subject.
>
> When Jo was a child her mother had warned her about the **germs she would catch** from reading other people's books. Jo's mother imagined **the unwashed and contaminated fingers** turning the pages, the **germs** mingling with the **sweat and grime** in some **toxic ferment** . . . a **dormant virus** waiting for the next unwary reader.
>
> . . . Jo conceded that there *were* some things you could **catch** from books and one of them was **Love** . . . There was nothing wrong with this, of course, in its place, but it could sometimes cause **complications**. It could sometimes **recur** in later life – like any **childhood disease** – in the more **virulent** form of Infatuation accompanied by its **terrible** sisters, Blind Folly and Delusion.
>
> Jo had first **caught the disease** at the age of ten from a novel by Georgette Heyer called *The Convenient Marriage*.
>
> (Bryers 2004: 30–31)

You might like to differentiate between the literal and the metaphorical in the above extract. Is it always possible to establish such a differentiation between metaphorical language and what appears to be literal language?

SUMMARY

In Chapter 1, we talked about the functions of metaphor and in this chapter we have looked at its role and purpose in literary texts. It has not been possible for us here to review the entire stock of creative devices that constitute figurative language in literature. We have, however, attempted to look at some of the principal ways in which writers have used, and use, this sort of language in their work. We have emphasized the importance of metaphor and of other tropes in the transmission of meaning from author to reader and the individuality of style that this involves.

To round off, read these extracts from Wilfred Owen and Seamus Heaney. First, from Owen, the first stanza of his 1918 poem, 'The Last Laugh':

> 'O Jesus Christ! I'm hit,' he said; and died.
> Whether he vainly cursed, or prayed indeed,
> The Bullets chirped – In vain! vain! vain!
> Machine-guns chuckled, – Tut-tut! Tut-tut!
> And the Big Gun guffawed.
>
> (Owen 1963: 59)

And second, from Seamus Heaney's 1966 poem, 'Digging':

> Between my finger and my thumb
> The squat pen rests; snug as a gun.
> (Heaney 1998: 3)

What tropes do Owen and Heaney make use of in these examples?

Remember, the importance of metaphorical language in literature is the scope it allows authors to exploit the possibilities of the language at their disposal and the questions that such exploitation creates in the minds of their readers.

FURTHER READING

Carter, R. (1998) *Vocabulary: Applied Linguistic Perspectives*, 2nd edn, London: Routledge. (Chapter 5, especially section 5.7.)

Gavins, J. and Steen, G. (eds) (2003) *Cognitive Poetics in Practice*. London: Routledge. (A collection of papers dealing with different aspects of figurative language in literary texts.)

Gibbs, R.W. (1994) *The Poetics of Mind: Figurative Thought, Language, and Understanding*, Cambridge: Cambridge University Press. (A cognitive approach.)

Kövecses, Z. (2002) *Metaphor: a Practical Introduction*, Oxford: Oxford University Press. (Chapter 4.)

Lakoff, G. and Turner, M. (1989) *More than Cool Reason: a Field Guide to Poetic Metaphor*, Chicago: University of Chicago Press. (Discussion of conceptual metaphors in literary texts.)

Lodge, D. (1977) *The Modes of Modern Writing: Metaphor, Metonymy, and the Typology of Modern Literature*, London: Edward Arnold.

Stockwell, P. (2002) *Cognitive Poetics: an Introduction*, London: Routledge. (Chapter 8 looks at conceptual metaphor.)

9

NON-VERBAL METAPHOR

We may read or hear a stretch of language, and we may pause because whoever is doing the writing or speaking may have used a particularly 'colourful' turn of phrase. They may have used words that realize a particularly creative metaphor. However, do metaphors have to be always expressed in language? Kövecses makes the point that 'if meta-phors are primarily conceptual, then they must realize themselves in other than linguistic ways' (2002: 52). More attention has of late been given to non-linguistic or non-verbal metaphor in areas such as acting, advertising, architecture, art, cartoons, colour symbolism, film, and theatre: sometimes there is overlap between two or more of these cate-gories. Kövecses devotes a chapter to this phenomenon, which includes the list above and other contexts which rely on means of interpretation that are not solely linguistic. Structurally, non-verbal metaphors may have verbal elements or co-occur with language; however, they may be entirely expressed through non-verbal means. We will be discus-sing examples of both types in this chapter, as we explore non-verbal metaphor in different media.

CINEMA

The world of cinema depends very much upon the verbal but films are also realized, very obviously, by the visual. Indeed, a complete film or different genres of films can be regarded as metaphors themselves. Over the last fifty years or so, the 'road movie' has become a distinctly recognizable genre. Such films often share features such as long highways going through the American West and disappearing into the distance: the impression, perhaps, is that they stretch into infinity. So we can again identify the LIFE IS A JOURNEY metaphor, with the road symbolizing life itself. Ridley Scott's 1991 film, *Thelma and Louise* is one such road movie where the two central female characters, initially 'escaping' for a weekend away from domestic monotony, are forced into crime after Louise shoots a would-be rapist. They become the pursued, and the chase takes place across the American Southwest which, in one sense, symbolizes freedom for the women as they flee into the desert, to the final symbol of ultimate freedom, when they drive over the edge of the Grand Canyon rather than face capture. There are many symbols of the American West here, and these include images of the genre of the western: for example, in the clothes worn by the men, jeans, hats, and boots, and the scene where cowboys drive cattle across the highway. The physical background to the narrative is filmed with an intensity of colour that heightens the viewer's perception of the metaphor. The American West has traditionally been considered a male, indeed macho-male, environment. As a result, the fact that the two protagonists of *Thelma and Louise* are women was seen by some as a symbol of female power in a male domain. Certainly, the majority of the male characters are amongst the least attractive of the entire cast.

The traditional western was for a long time a well-established genre in Hollywood (by traditional western, we mean those which precede the films of directors such as Peckinpah, Leone, and Eastwood). In traditional westerns, metaphor and metonymy are used to draw clear distinctions between good and bad. For example, symbols such as white hats and black hats realize who is 'good' and who is 'bad'. The fact that the majority of these films were shot in black and white adds a further dimension. Other symbols of the genre are horses and guns. The former symbolize freedom of movement in the American West, and the latter justice and the American citizen's right to self-defence. Furthermore, if the horses or guns were used by a 'white hat', justice would prevail, as opposed to evil if used by a 'black hat'.

The *Lord of the Rings* films provide further manifestations of non-verbal metaphor on the big screen. We have several recurring elements or symbols: for example, the hero, whom we observe setting out on a journey or quest and whom we accompany on that quest, along with his faithful companion or companions; they must endure grave perils before overcoming the forces of evil. Colour is important here, as darkness in a number of ways realizes evil, and white or other lighter colours realize good. The Orcs, for example, are depicted as being dark and swarthy as well as slant-eyed. Frodo and his friends have to travel from the Shire, which is symbolic of innocence and stability, to the Land of Mordor and the Dark Lord Sauron, who represents evil. One of the most important symbols is, of course, the Ring. It is a metaphor for evil and corrupt power. Indeed, so strong is the influence of the Ring on whoever carries it that it is almost as if it has agency, that it is another 'character' in the narrative. Overall, the whole sequence of the *Lord of the Rings* narratives and films can be seen as a metaphor for Good versus Evil.

MUSIC

In the world of cinema, music has an important role, and it too can realize non-verbal metaphor. In *Thelma and Louise*, for example, the music as the credits roll is of a country-and-western type that we would associate with the western United States. The background music matches vision in further underpinning metaphorical and symbolic meanings.

Many composers think, or thought, of pieces of music in terms of colour: Liszt frequently used colour vocabulary when describing his music, and the linkage between language, music, and colour is effectively a triangular metaphor (we will look further at colour and music later). Other composers see music as symbolizing personal characteristics. Elton John's 'Candle in the Wind', originally written as a tribute to Marilyn Monroe and then rewritten in memory of Diana, Princess of Wales, is one such. Both the verbal title and lyrics and the non-verbal musical accompaniment can be said to complement each other as metaphorical elements in realizing the fragility of life. Staying with the image of 'the wind', Christopher Guest's film *A Mighty Wind* satirizes the folk-music scene deriving from the early 1960s. The title song of the film is 'The Mighty Wind', but the 'wind' featured in several 1960s songs was the 'wind of change', socially, politically, and sexually, that was 'blowing' through the United States. Bob Dylan's song 'Blowing in the Wind' probably encapsulates the symbolism of those changes more than most.

Sound itself, of course, has a role as non-verbal metaphor. In the field of electro-acoustic music, sounds are the material composers use to create images, to realize concepts. Jonty Harrison is to the fore as a major composer in this genre. Harrison, who has a chair in music at the University of Birmingham, has described one of the principal source sounds for his piece *Hot Air*. This source was balloons from a children's party which he says 'gives rise to a train of thought which, after linking "toy" balloons to "hot air" balloons, went on to draw in other concepts of air (breath, utterance, and natural phenomena) and heat (energy, action, danger)' (Harrison 2002). These concepts are realized by 'a shift of focus away from instrumental generalizations' to compositions where 'the musical forms are no longer abstract, but abstracted from . . . recognisable sounds. The sounds of our every day experience' (Harrison 1996: 16). The result of the synthesized sonic composition *Hot Air* was, Harrison says, to reveal 'another, altogether more worrying image: that of the inflated balloon as a metaphor of the very environment of the Earth itself' (Harrison 2002).

PICTORIAL REPRESENTATION

Pictorial metaphor is one non-verbal form which has received a lot of attention over the last few years. In a recent Turner exhibition (*Turner in Britain*), the earlier landscapes and later seascapes provide interesting examples. In both, the viewer's perspective is to be always looking towards the horizon. In later life, of course, this is symbolic of looking towards death. Thus, the LIFE IS A JOURNEY metaphor is realized in a particular visual or non-verbal way.

We discussed verbal metaphor and literature in Chapter 8. Peter Crisp (2003: 100) points out how non-verbal metaphor can be realized in literary texts. He cites the illustrations in Dickens's novels and the poems of William Blake as two examples. In children's literature, Quentin Blake's illustrations for Roald Dahl's work fulfil a similar non-verbal function. Blake's caricatures can be seen as non-linguistic metaphorical complements to Dahl's characterizations, a necessary component of his fantasy of the grotesque. Blake's drawing of Miss Trunchbull in *Matilda* is an excellent example of this, as are his illustrations of Matilda's father and mother.

Photography, while it captures reality, can also present images for interpretation. Diane Arbus, the well-known American photographer who died in 1971, was of the view that people do not necessarily see the same thing or experience the same 'reality'. Some of Arbus's best-known work is to be found in her photographs of anonymous people in New York's Central Park. The faces of her subjects present a whole range of emotions: anger, fear, admiration, and so on, as only people's expressions can. In fact, as Lakoff and Johnson (1980/2003: 37) point out, faces as metonyms are very much a part of our culture in both photography and painting. According to Liz Jobey (*The Guardian*, 10 January 2004), Arbus and her contemporary Robert Frank were 'seeing symbols, finding metaphors for the state of the world around them'. Jobey refers to one particularly famous photograph of Robert Frank's. This is the image of the white line stretching down the highway to infinity. This can suggest, on the one hand, 'hope, ambition, expectation'; on the other, 'disillusion, stasis, failure'. The image is also central to the road movies we looked at earlier, or Turner's paintings: LIFE IS A JOURNEY once again.

In Chapter 7, we saw how advertising depends very much not only on the slogan and the body copy but also on pictorial images. Indeed, some advertisements have little linguistic content at all, but rely almost solely on the *image*. The majority, however, have both elements. In the *Observer Magazine* (23 November 2003), there was an advertisement for a Nokia mobile phone. There is quite a lot of text here, but the visual element dominates. It is a full-page glossy photograph of a highly confident young businessman. He is foregrounded and has a determined expression and appears to be striding purposefully forward. Next to him is a picture of the Nokia 6600. The verbal element (the 'sales pitch') is contained in ten noun phrases, which are superimposed in a circle on the man's breast pocket surrounding the sub-heading *Vision*. The indication is that the phone, with all its many functions, can be easily carried in that pocket. All this in such a tiny space! A multi-faceted tool for a multi-talented and upwardly mobile young businessman. A man with *vision*. Another sub-heading, *Reality*, is located above the image of the phone and close to the picture of the man. The verbal element is obviously important but the advertisement requires the visual to achieve impact. This advertisement contains an interesting example of what Forceville (1998: 126–127) refers to as MP2s or 'metaphors with two pictorially present terms'. One of these is primary and the other secondary. The Nokia 6600 is the primary subject of our metaphor. It is the *reality*.

Interestingly, in *The Observer*'s sister paper, *The Guardian*, of the day before we have exactly the same advertisement. However, the character foregrounded pictorially is a young woman (*Guardian* (*Weekend*), 22 November 2003). Again, the subject appears to be striding forward with great self-assurance. Again, we see the same noun phrases or bullet points surrounding *Vision* but in this case superimposed on the woman's handbag. Like her male colleague, she may have the *vision* but must rely on the Nokia 6600 for *Reality*, the reality that will ensure her success. One of the slogans in the two versions of this advertisement summarizes the metaphor, VISION BECOMES/IS REALITY: that metaphor which underpins the equation of seeing and knowledge/truth in Western cultures.

There is another, highly significant dimension to the Nokia metaphor. The non-verbal element of the advertisement relies on colour to help achieve full impact. The man is dressed in a very well tailored two-piece suit in pale blue with a blue tie and the background is also a hazy shade of light blue. The same highly significant degree of 'blueness' is very evident in *The Guardian* advertisement. Blue is also the predominant colour at three important stages of the verbal element, where the product, Nokia, is named three times using blue typeface. The choice of colour is interesting here, as colours can be seen as crossovers between verbal and non-verbal metaphors. There is a long history of colours being associated with emotions and blue is associated with calmness and peace: it can also be associated with truth. Presumably, the acquisition of this mobile phone will complement the young executives' working lifestyles. In other words, although busy and determined, they will also be calm and truthful in decision-making with their 'partner' the Nokia 6600. So, if it can do it for them, it can do it for you. The visual element communicates with the reader just as effectively as the verbal. It is a good example of what Kress and van Leeuwen refer to as the 'overwhelming evidence of the importance of visual communication' (1996: 16).

Another point of interest is that an internet advertisement for the same product, the Nokia 6600, has a predominance of blue highlighting the background. We will return to colours later in this chapter.

NOTICES AND SIGNS

One of the most common, day-to-day manifestations of non-verbal metaphor is realized in notices and signs in the world around us.

We are helped to navigate unfamiliar – and familiar – places through our knowledge that certain symbols have certain meanings. A sign with a cup represents a snack bar; arrows on signs indicate which direction we are to follow. While they appear to be a very ordinary part of everyday life, they are, nevertheless, of interest, and important (think of symbols for emergency exits).

Related to these are signals to road-users by other drivers and in traffic signs. There are, of course, some very obvious ones. Direction Indicator Signals, for example, are exactly what they say: the use of mechanical devices such as flashing amber lights to indicate turning left or right, or red brake lights to indicate that a driver is slowing down. Arm signals can also be used as indicators of direction, and are mainly used by cyclists and horse-riders to communicate that they are turning right or left.

The British Government's Highway Code lists various categories of road sign, and colours are important here too. Signs giving orders are presented within a red circle: as the Highway Code says, 'Signs with red circles are mostly prohibitive.' In zones where there are restrictions on speed, signs will have the miles per hour numerically presented on a white background within a red circle. 'Give way' signs are red triangles with the instruction GIVE WAY contained within the triangle on a white background. STOP AND GIVE WAY signs are red octagonals with the command in white with a red background. The 'no overtaking' sign has no verbal component, but is completely realized as a symbol: a red-bordered circle with a black car on the left and a red car on the right. Manually-operated signs at roadworks have STOP signs very similar to the STOP AND GIVE WAY sign, while the GO sign, on the other hand, is white lettering imposed on a green circle.

Other colours are also employed prohibitively. White lines across British roads at junctions are used to reinforce the message that motorists must stop at a stop sign. White lines of different types running the lengths of roads indicate the boundaries of traffic lines and whether it is permissible or not to overtake. Yellow or red lines along the edges of roads help reinforce the meanings conveyed by signs which indicate whether and when it is possible to park.

While red is prohibitive, British road signs with blue circles and no red border nearly always convey positive information for certain categories of road-user. So, a white bicycle on a blue circle means 'pedal cycles only'. A blue circle with a white bicycle above a white bus and the word ONLY suspended from the circle means 'buses and cycles only'.

Road signs with images of cars and other vehicles can be considered metonymic. Many other road signs also represent metonyms. For example, on brown tourist information signs, a carousel represents a theme or amusement park: similarly, a football represents a football ground, an elephant a zoo, a duck a nature reserve, and a stylized flower a garden. Compare the symbols used on maps: a tankard to represent a pub, a receiver for a public phone, and a triangular flag on a stick for a golf course.

There are other public signs in our culture which convey non-verbal meaning. In Britain, pub signs are a very visual example and often are realizations of life in the past. Thus, a pub called 'The Coach and Horses' will have a sign with a coach and horses and could well have been an old coaching inn. Pubs or inns were often local landmarks, and an illiterate local peasantry could give directions to strangers by using the visual dimension: a pub sign or a building such as a church. In rural England, pubs were often sited close to churches, which is one reason why many pubs are called 'The Bell'. (Church bells themselves were symbolic realizations of the passing of time for a country community.) There are other rural pub signs, such as 'Fox and Hounds' referring to hunting, or 'George and Dragon' based on the legend of England's patron saint and his killing of the dragon. One relic of a mythical past is the pub sign 'The Green Man'. The Green Man is actually a symbol from pre-Christian times: a forest-dwelling spirit whose face was supposedly sometimes seen when looking closely at the foliage of trees and bushes deep in woodland, and who, although a pagan figure, was sometimes carved on the outside of medieval churches. City pub signs too can realize famous buildings such as 'The Edinburgh Castle', or other historical symbols such as ships, hence 'The Cutty Sark' in Greenwich, London. Imperialism is also catered for with pub signs with the figure of Britannia representing 'The Britannia Inn', or a picture of Queen Victoria for a pub of the same name.

COLOUR AND COLOUR SYMBOLISM

It is probably apparent by now that colour can be an important dimension in the conveying of non-verbal meaning. We said earlier that colours might be considered as examples of crossovers between verbal and non-verbal metaphor. The symbolism inherent in so many colours is, therefore, a very significant factor for a great many people.

National flags are probably one of the most common realizations of non-verbal colour metaphor. The national flag of England is the St George's cross; a red cross on a white background. The flag is an icon for English sports fans though it has also been associated with those on the political right in English politics. Indeed, a British educational journal, the *Times Educational Supplement* (7 May 2004), carried an article concerning a teacher who was allegedly a member of a political party of the far right, the British National Party (BNP). Accompanying the article was a picture of a BNP rally with numerous flags of St George. The shaven heads of the marchers might also be interpreted as a metonym for supporters of their political beliefs. Compare the use of colours in military uniforms – for example, the blue of Union soldiers and the grey of the Confederates in the American Civil War (as in *We answer to no grey South / Nor blue North* in the poem by Paul Muldoon, cited in Chapter 2).

Numbers and shapes can complement colours. The national flag of the United States, the Stars and Stripes, has fifty stars representing all the states in the Union. The thirteen stripes symbolize the thirteen original states, formerly British colonies. The French tricolour's red, white, and blue were associated with the Revolutionaries of 1789. However, Pierre Gay (1998), contributing to a French web site, has pointed out that the meanings of the colours are now associated with different, 'invented' origins. The red signifies St Denis, the patron saint of Paris; the white, the Virgin Mary and also Joan of Arc, who drove the English out of France; and the blue is for St Martin, who cut his blue cloak in half so that he could give one half to a freezing beggar.

Colours, of course, have other, more subtle connotations. Consider, for example, the relationship between colour and emotion. *Astonishing Splashes of Colour* by Clare Morrall was shortlisted for the Man Booker Prize in 2003. In her novel, Morrall addresses the concept of seeing emotions as colours. 'The people outside the school gates are yellow because of their optimism' (2003: 9), says the narrator, who also dreams in colours:

> I dream in colours, astonishing, shimmering, clashing colours. So many shades. Not just red, but crimson, vermilion, scarlet, rose. There are not enough names

for the colours in my dreams. I wake up longing for visual silence, looking for a small dark place where there is no light.

(Morrall 2003: 35)

The reader is not told here what the 'reds' symbolize but context suggests disturbing rather than peaceful emotions. Red itself can have negative connotations, as in the following expressions:

To be **in the red**

To **see red**

To be **red with rage**

Compare too the conceptual metaphors relating to heat, fire, and redness: EMOTION IS HEAT or EMOTION IS FIRE, as in

Susan was extremely angry, she was absolutely **burning** with resentment after John's behaviour at the party.

Bill and Tom really are **red-hot** Socialists.

We have already commented on blue and its positive significance in advertising and British road signs. In an article entitled 'And in the blue corner . . .' Sean Coughlan (*The Guardian*, 17 January 2004) comments on the association between British banks and colour. Again, we see the red/blue contrast. After all, the expression *in the red* signifies debt. One British bank, the Abbey National (now Abbey), redecorated some of its branches in blue and using pink lettering for its name, rather than its traditional red and white. About a dozen banks and building societies use blue in their branches: the British bank Lloyds/TSB use blue and green. Coughlan quotes a psychologist who points out that blue is associated with calm (as we mentioned earlier), and blue and green together assist in putting people at their ease. Red, he says, is 'associated with aggression and risk'. Another psychologist, quoted in the same article, supports this view and he points out 'that the power of the visual memory is much stronger than anything from any spoken or written message'.

Red, of course, is associated with anger and rage, as expressed in the ANGER IS HEAT/FIRE metaphors. It can also signify extreme sexual desire, and this is realized non-verbally through the SEXUAL DESIRE IS FIRE metaphor. Kövecses (2002: 57–58) cites the Disney production *The Hunchback of Notre Dame* in exemplification. In one scene, the judge is overwhelmed by sexual desire for Esmeralda and the whole palace becomes covered in flames. Another example can be found in Ken Russell's 1969 film version of D.H. Lawrence's *Women in Love*: the famous – for many at the time, infamous – scene in which Oliver Reed and Alan Bates wrestle naked in front of a roaring fire.

We have already mentioned colour in relation to symbols and cinema. Many films are noted for an important use of colour in their cinematography as well as in the design of sets and costume. Even in the days of black and white films, patterns of light and shadow created meaning, not just visual effect: a good example of this is film noir. Amongst recent cinematographers who are associated with a strong use of colour is Christopher Doyle, who has worked with Asian directors such as Zhang Yimou and Wong Kar-wai. In the 2002 film *Hero*, for example, different phases of the film are themed by different colours: a sword fight between two female warriors takes place against a backdrop of golden leaves and light, which turns red as the fight climaxes; the attempted assassination at the end happens in a hall hung with billowing green banners, which seem to be choreographed along with the ensuing fight.

Earlier in this chapter, we commented on composers who think of pieces of music as colours. Sir Isaac Newton was probably the first to associate sound and colour. He correlated musical notes with colours so that the seven notes of the musical scale matched or corresponded with the spectrum of colours that constitute sunlight as reflected by a prism: these are the colours used to describe the rainbow. Newton represented this correlation in diagrammatic form with his 'Colour Musical Wheel' in his *Opticks*, first published in 1704. This 'wheel' was actually a circle divided into segments. Each segment represented one colour of the spectrum in order – Red, Orange, Yellow, Green, Blue, Indigo, Violet. On the outer rim or circumference of the circle are the seven notes of the musical scale with the segments coming between them. Thus, the Red segment occurs between D and E. Newton used D as the starting point for the white note scale on a keyboard.

STATUES, MONUMENTS, AND CULTURAL SYMBOLS

Public art such as statues typically has symbolic value: this is also true of monuments and other memorial structures. Kövecses (2002: 59) comments on how the symbols may often be based on metaphors, which are culturally significant, and cites as an example the Statue of Liberty in New York. This, he says, 'was created to evoke the idea that liberty was achieved in the United States (together with its "accompaniments" – knowledge and justice)'. He identifies several metaphors in the statue as symbol, and he sums up his analysis by saying 'the statue may be regarded as an embodiment of the metaphorical source domains: UNINHIBITED MOVEMENT, MOVEMENT FROM DARK TO LIGHT, and SEEING'.

Statues, of course, may be symbols based on a culture, which many find to be alien in terms of history. For many years, in the centre of Dublin, Ireland, there stood a statue known as Nelson's Pillar. This statue, in memory of the hero of the Battle of Trafalgar, had Nelson standing sword in hand at the top of his pillar, evoking a metaphor for the triumph of Nelson and the Royal Navy in particular and the might of the British Empire in general. Over a century later, the statue was destroyed by a militant political organization, who presumably interpreted this symbol rather differently. In fact, their action in itself can be seen as the metaphor HISTORICAL CHANGE IS MOVEMENT FROM A STATE OF IGNORANCE TO A STATE OF KNOWLEDGE (see Kövecses 2002: 59). Close to where Nelson's Pillar used to stand is a building, which realizes a very important historical symbolism for many Irish people: this is Dublin's General Post Office. The Post Office was occupied by armed men on Easter Monday 1916, and marks the beginning of the rebellion which led to the independence of twenty-six of Ireland's thirty-two counties a few years later.

Kövecses (2002: 63) points out that in one metaphorical system of morality, BEING GOOD IS UPRIGHT and BEING BAD IS BEING LOW. In the war against Iraq, Saddam Hussein had to be 'toppled' and this was symbolically realized in the pulling down of his many statues throughout the country. Ironically, during President Bush's state visit to London in November 2003, demonstrators 'toppled' a plastic statue of the President. This symbol could be observed by television viewers as a non-verbal action, and delivered verbally by a newsreader actually using the lexical item *toppled*.

Other countries have other objects as metaphors. The Arc de Triomphe in Paris is one example: a monument in which there are sculptures and other symbols. These symbols include the grave of the Unknown Soldier, a permanently burning flame of remembrance and, on national days, a flag which is draped through the arch. Buildings themselves can be seen as a type of non-verbal metaphor: we will not discuss metaphor in architecture here, but we give suggestions for further reading at the end of this chapter.

Flags, as we have seen, are symbols that can evoke certain feelings. To return to Ireland: in Northern Ireland, it is not unusual to travel through a part of the Province where the tricolour (national flag of the Irish Republic) can be seen flying from telegraph poles with, very often, the kerb stones painted in the colours of that flag; green, white, and orange (the colours themselves are potently symbolic). A little later, the traveller might well see the Union Flag (the national flag of the United Kingdom) accompanied by red, white, and blue kerb stones. The former symbolizes the feelings of many Nationalist citizens and the latter of many Unionists or 'Loyalists'. The gable walls at the end of working-class terraced streets in Belfast often have quite elaborate murals depicting scenes from Irish history or the recent 'Troubles'. These symbols will indicate to the passer-by the political affiliations of the local residents. (There is a certain irony here in that these are now fast becoming a tourist attraction.) Finally, rather different symbols from Ireland are to be found within the Police Service for Northern Ireland. This police force was set up to replace the Royal Ulster Constabulary (RUC) which for many in one of the two main communities was a symbol of oppression. The new force not only has a new name but a new cap badge and a new motto. Furthermore, police cars are now painted in colours similar to those to be found in the rest of Great Britain. Again, these are examples of the way in which non-verbal metaphor can be utilized for the purposes of propaganda. In the case of the police symbols they were created in the attempt 'to win hearts and minds' (a linguistic metonym, of course).

RELIGION

Religious institutions have long been seen as the guardians of a country's morals. As such, religion plays a major part in the day-to-day life of many people, and notably at times of great danger. The military funerals of British servicemen killed in the Second Gulf War and afterwards provide an evocative symbol of this: the uniforms, the flag-draped coffins, the slow march, and sometimes regimental music of a suitably sombre type. Interestingly enough, the televising of military funerals is not permitted in some countries. Is this a fear on behalf of the authorities that such scenes might persuade people to question the activities of their country's troops? Why are soldiers being killed? What is the morality of this? The very absence of such televised reports can itself be seen as a non-verbal metaphor, capable of interpretation in several ways.

As we have already seen, concepts of HIGH/UP and LOW/DOWN are used metaphorically in relation to good and evil, morality and immorality. We have, in the Christian religion at least, the concept of the fallen angel, and throughout history Hell has been conceived of as being 'down there' and Heaven 'up there': compare our discussion in Chapter 7. Britain is often regarded as not being a church-attending nation. However, while this may be so in terms of the established Christian Church, religion is still regarded as enshrining morality, and reinforcing the metaphors EVIL IS A FORCE and MORALITY IS A STRENGTH (see Kövecses 2002: 63). This reinforcement is executed both verbally and non-verbally. Furthermore, it should not be forgotten that Britain is now a multi-faith society, with all the major world religions and guardians of morality represented. The United States, of course, is also a strongly religious country.

In Christianity, two of the most well-known symbols are the bread and wine used in the service of Holy Communion: the body and blood of Christ. Perhaps the best-known Christian symbol of all is the cross itself upon which Christ was crucified. Variations of this have become symbols of something a lot more sinister, such as the fiery cross of the Ku Klux Klan which persecuted and often murdered black Americans in the southern United States: compare the swastika, a form of cross, which was originally a symbol of good luck, but is now associated with Nazi Germany and fascism.

One metaphorical, non-verbal realization which Christianity shares with other world religions is that of the significance of water. Here, both history and myth combine. For the Christian, water which is blessed and therefore pure symbolizes baptism and acceptance into the faith when the priest makes the sign of the cross upon the forehead of the candidate. It thus represents the beginning of LIFE IS A JOURNEY both spiritually and physically for the infant, and spiritually for the adult. Some Christians see so much significance in the symbol of water that baptism means total immersion.

In Islam, regular bathing symbolizes the unity of body and soul, belief in which is a basic tenet of that faith and is a religious requirement for the very notion of worship. According to Islam, all natural, unpolluted water is clean and is a gift from God. Unlike Christianity, it requires no special blessing.

For members of the Jewish faith, water represents purity, and the mikveh is a ritual bath of natural water for cleansing after menstruation or in the initiation rites for converts or after contact with a dead body. Priests too had to wash their hands and feet before taking part in services in the Temple. The washing of hands before and after meals is also an important ritual washing.

In Hinduism, where a system of beliefs is based on an intimate relationship with nature, rivers are sacred. The River Ganges is probably the most sacred and Benares, sited on the banks of that river, is a place of pilgrimage.

Buddhism, too, values water. Water symbolizes clarity and calmness. For Buddhists water is a reminder to cleanse the mind and acquire a state of purity.

SUMMARY

Non-verbal metaphor, as we have seen, can take a variety of forms and ranges across a spectrum of representation: film, music, painting, photography, religion, public art, and even road signs. We could have written a book on non-verbal metaphor alone, and there are areas and contexts which space has not permitted us to investigate. Gesture is one, and this includes sign language. Consider, too, the work of the British actor and satirist John Cleese in his representation of Basil Fawlty in *Fawlty Towers* or, more recently, Jennifer Saunders and Joanna Lumley in *Absolutely Fabulous*. All three performers achieved much of their success not only because of what they said but also because of their ability to exaggerate their body language. In other words, parts of their body, their facial expressions, and so on can become non-verbal realizations of happiness, anger, or embarrassment. In the context of comedy, exaggerated movements 'speak', and if we think of circus clowns or Charlie Chaplin's silent movies, we have two excellent examples where communication relies on the manipulation of the non-verbal metaphor. The clowns and Chaplin use mime, and that mime, after all, is farce based on real life using mimicry. Think also of pantomimes like *Mother Goose* and *Cinderella*. Equally, in ballet, we have the conveyance of meaning by both movement and music working together to present a story that may involve one or more themes. The point is both music and dance can convey metaphor, and they are well worth exploring further because of this.

FURTHER READING

Caballero, R. (2003) 'Metaphor and genre: the presence and role of metaphor in the building review', *Applied Linguistics* 24/2: 145–167. (Investigates the use of metaphorical language in writing about architecture.)

Forceville, C. (1998) *Pictorial Metaphor in Advertising*, London: Routledge.

Forty, A. (2000; paperback edn 2004) *Words and Buildings: A Vocabulary of Modern Architecture*, London: Thames and Hudson. (Discusses the relationship between architecture and language: Chapters 4 and 5 deal specifically with metaphor.)

Kövecses, Z. (2002) *Metaphor: a Practical Introduction*, Oxford: Oxford University Press. (Chapter 5.)

Vestergaard, T. and Schrøder, K. (1985) *The Language of Advertising*. Oxford: Blackwell. (Chapter 2 on the visual image.)

10

CODA

At the beginning of Chapter 1, we said that the intention of this book was to introduce the study of metaphor, and to show how and why it is important. We could not hope to cover the topic exhaustively, but we hoped to bridge the gap — another metaphor — between brief discussions in general linguistics books and the detailed discussions of specialist texts: to outline sufficiently the principal aspects of the topic and then to describe how figurative language is used in a variety of linguistic and non-verbal contexts. We have given some suggestions for further reading at the end of each chapter, after summarizing our main points, and we give suggestions for small-scale student investigations of figurative language in our appendix 'Researching metaphor'.

We could have called this short final chapter a conclusion. But the word *conclusion* suggests a completion, or perhaps a final rational judgement based on an assessment of the available evidence: *conclude* and *conclusion* themselves derive from the Latin verb *claudere* 'shut'. It seemed important to us to emphasize that the study of metaphor, whether theoretical or practical, is open-ended, and that this book is just a beginning for that process.

So instead we have chosen the word *coda* as title: a musical term for a passage at the end of a piece, derived via Italian from Latin *cauda* 'tail', and so itself metaphorical. In linguistics, Labov's model of the structure of oral narratives uses *coda* to refer to a section at the end of a narrative, containing general observations or linking the narrative to the time of narration (see Labov 1972: 363ff.). In dance, the coda of a ballet is a finale in which the principal dancers reappear. For our coda, we simply offer some further examples of metaphor for consideration.

Contestants in TV shows in which they undergo an extended period of intensive training, competing for a recording contract or other such prize, commonly use the metaphor *journey* to refer to their experiences. 'It has been such a journey', they say; commentators talk of obstacles on a contestant's 'journey'. Does the use of this metaphor shift attention from the material goals of fame and money to personal development? Does it make participation in what might be considered just shallow entertainment seem serious and worthwhile?

The following is the opening of a poem, 'The Second Voyage', by the Irish poet, Eiléan Ní Chuilleanáin:

> Odysseus rested on his oar and saw
> The ruffled foreheads of the waves
> Crocodiling and mincing past: he rammed
> The oar between their jaws and looked down
> In the simmering sea where scribbles of weed defined
> Uncertain depth, and the slim fishes progressed
> In fatal formation . . .
>
> (Ní Chuilleanáin 1986: 26)

What kinds of image do these forceful and startling metaphors generate? How do they convey the writer's meanings? What are those meanings?

The Nigerian writer Chinua Achebe's novel *Things Fall Apart* deals with the effect of colonization on the Ibo in the nineteenth century. A new, European, minister arrives at a newly-established missionary church, with a particular world view:

> He saw things as black and white. And black was evil. He saw the world as a battlefield in which the children of light were locked in mortal combat with the sons of darkness. He spoke in his sermons about sheep and goats and about wheat and tares. He believed in slaying the prophets of Baal.
>
> (Achebe 1958/2001: 134)

Here and later on in this chapter, Achebe uses biblical metaphors to refer ironically to the minister and his work. But what particular effect is created by the use in this context of the traditional conceptual metaphors LIGHT/WHITE IS GOOD, DARK/BLACK IS EVIL?

The metaphor *road map* is used in various political and economic contexts: in particular, the phrase *road map to peace* has been used by Tony Blair and other world leaders to refer to the strategies suggested by Western governments for resolving conflict in the Middle East, particularly in relation to that between Palestinians and Israelis. Why has this metaphor been used instead of a word such as *strategy*, *plan*, or *suggestion*, or even a technology-grounded metaphor such as *blueprint*? In this particular situation, does it imply not just that peace can be achieved but that it is possible to see how to achieve it, because the best 'route' has already been set down? Who set it down?

At the time of writing, it seems that over 250,000 people died in the Indian Ocean earthquake and subsequent tsunami of December 2004. Commentators have drawn parallels with the catastrophic eruption of Krakatoa in 1883: one contrast made is that people widely realize that geological processes caused the tsunami, whereas in 1883 the disaster was attributed by many to supernatural agencies, or seen as divine punishment. While Western television reporters were quite properly muted in their descriptions of the immediate post-tsunami situation, it was noticeable that many personified the tsunami: *the vicious surge of water*; *[people] will never be able to forget the day the ocean turned on them*; *the ocean is calm now, after its fit of raging temper, but it has already done its worst*. Was this just journalistic rhetoric? Or does it suggest that, in spite of twenty-first-century scientific rationalism, there was a deep-seated feeling that blame, not just explanation, was required?

Lastly, the 1930 American film *All Quiet on the Western Front*, based on a book by Erich Maria Remarque, deals with the 1914–1918 war from the perspective of a young German recruit. He is initially idealistic, later disillusioned. In the famous closing sequence, he is in a battlefield trench. Reaching up out of it towards a butterfly, he is shot and killed. The butterfly is real, but also symbolic. Is it a metaphor for life? Hope? Transience? Futility? Or all of these things and more?

These final examples, we hope, will underline the importance of the study of metaphor, its richness, and its interest.

APPENDIX

Researching metaphor

This appendix suggests some ways for students to explore metaphor practically: you may, of course, have already had ideas about what to do next. For our own part, we believe that it is important to work from data, whether that data is drawn from informant testing, is derived from a corpus, consists of a text or group of texts, or is based on other sources of data such as scholarly dictionaries.

A starting-point might be the kind of text from which we quoted in Chapter 1: travel writing or restaurant criticism. Such texts typically make extensive use of figurative language in order to describe what the writer has experienced, to create or re-create atmosphere, and to communicate evaluations, whether positive or negative. Identify the figurative language in the text, and analyse what its effects are. How overt and how clear are the overall description and evaluation? To what extent are you, as reader, encouraged to agree with the writer through his or her choice of metaphor?

One of the simplest ways to examine metaphor and metonymy in relation to word meaning is to select a highly polysemous word – find a 'long' entry in a dictionary, perhaps a noun. Which of its different senses reflect metaphorical processes and how would you explain the metaphors? Which reflect metonymic ones? Now look at a verb or adjective, or a grammatical item such as *under*, and consider *its* metaphors. The *Oxford English Dictionary* provides information about the historical development of senses: check to see how your analysis fits with this, and whether there are other, obsolete senses which also fit in. Etymological dictionaries give information about the roots of words (as does the *Oxford English Dictionary*), from which it is possible to detect metaphor further. If you are interested in metaphorical idioms and proverbs, there are a number of reference books which include explanations of their origins: reliable sources include the specialist dictionaries published by Oxford University Press, and *Brewer's Dictionary of Phrase and Fable*.

Most investigations of conceptual metaphor use linguistic realizations to exemplify mappings, although they may start with concepts. We have discussed a number of conceptual metaphors in this book, and you could choose one of these to explore and map out fully. Alternatively, you could choose to focus on a particular domain, either target or source. For ideas, there is a web site for conceptual metaphor at <http://cogsci.berkeley.edu/lakoff/>, which lists a large number of metaphors and indexes both target and source domains. Many of the metaphors have relatively few linguistic realizations: see whether you can find more. However, there is no straightforward source from which to draw further examples. If you want to investigate a target domain, one technique is to use a thesaurus – perhaps an alphabetically-organized thesaurus, rather than a traditional thematically-organized thesaurus such as Roget's. Then look up entries for central terms within that domain: for example, if you are investigating ANGER or PURPOSE, look up *angry*, *anger*, *furious*, *rage*, or *purpose*, *aim*, *intend*, *intention*. Which of the listed synonyms express particular concepts, or relate to particular source domains? Some, such as idioms, will be obvious; others less so. If the listed synonyms include more formal Latinate words, check their etymologies to see whether, historically, they represent the same conceptual metaphor. To investigate a source domain, a similar technique is to consider the polysemy of common, central terms, what metaphorical senses they have, and to what target domains they relate. For example, to investigate WAR/STRUGGLE, look at words such as *attack* and *fight*: use an idioms dictionary to find metaphorical expressions which fit in. (Another useful resource is Alice Deignan's thematic dictionary of metaphors (1995): each chapter covers a source domain such as 'animals', 'cooking and food', or 'light, darkness, and colour', explaining metaphorical usages of items within the domain.)

As you are doing this, ask yourself whether your work makes you more, or less, convinced of the validity of claims about conceptual metaphor. Is it just random coincidence that a semantic set of words maps similarly onto a domain, or is it systematic?

Scientific psycholinguistic investigations of metaphor and the brain are beyond the scope of most general researchers. On a much smaller scale, however, it is possible to acquire useful data through more informal informant testing. The mental images which people have of idiom metaphors, when introspecting, is one possible topic: what image do your friends, co-students, or family have for *spill the beans* (see Chapter 5), or for idioms such as *fight fire with fire*, *a wet blanket*, *pull the plug on something*, or *toe the line*? Are there any observable differences between age groups or genders? Similarly, to what extent do informants agree about the meanings and implication of metaphors in a short text, such as a poem, newspaper editorial, or review?

If you have access to a corpus, such as the British National Corpus, then you already have access to a vast amount of primary data. It is possible to learn a lot simply by looking to see how a particular metaphorical word or phrase is used (compare our comments in Chapter 5). What kinds of text does the word or phrase appear in, what are the relative proportions of literal and metaphorical uses, and are there any differences between them in terms of collocates? You could investigate a thematic set of items, ones which realize a conceptual metaphor. For example, we conceptualize malice and resentment in terms of poison and destruction (*poisonous*, *venomous*, *toxic*, *gnaw/eat away at*), and difficulties as if they are knots or tangles (*knotty*, *tied up in knots*, *unravel*, *disentangle*, *tease out*). Compare how they are used: are some items used metaphorically more often than others?

If you are bilingual, you may want to compare metaphor in your two languages. How far do they share a conceptual metaphor, such as ANGER IS HEAT or ARGUMENT IS WAR/STRUGGLE? Does your other language conceptualize anger in that way or in another? And does it provide support for the contention by Lakoff and Johnson that UP/DOWN metaphors seem to be universal? You could perhaps compare a translation of a literary text with the original, or even try translating a metaphor-rich text from your second language into your first: how many metaphors cross over, how many do not? If you are not bilingual, but you have friends or co-students whose first language is not English, you could ask them about how they interpret the metaphors in a text, and what their mental images are. Are there distinctions between what they say, and your own intuitions as a native speaker?

Chapter 7 dealt with metaphor in relation to evaluation and ideology. It is easy to collect data to explore this, and newspapers are one obvious source. Compare the differences between the metaphors used by more conservative and more liberal papers, or between broadsheets and tabloids: limit the variables by restricting yourself to one kind of text (editorials, human interest stories, arts reviews) or to a day's top story. Election leaflets and other political materials are another useful source. Parties typically construct a 'we good/they bad' contrast in their output, as propaganda: can you find evidence that metaphor is used to convey, perhaps subliminally, this contrast? Similarly, it is easy to collect data to explore how metaphor is used in relation to social activities. For sports, fanzines and newspaper reports provide written data: again, it is worth factoring in differences between broadsheets and tabloids. You could also tape radio or television commentaries: what metaphors are used? Are there any differences, say, between British commentary on soccer matches, and American commentary on baseball or ice hockey games? If you want to look at advertising, then limit the variables by considering a particular type of product (cars, cosmetics, food . . .) and taking into account its target demographic. Analyse the linguistic metaphors and other figurative language; but also analyse the non-verbal metaphors in the images in the advertisements, and consider how linguistic and non-verbal metaphors interact.

Chapter 8 looked at literary metaphor and other kinds of figurative language. Most of our examples were drawn from children's literature and popular fiction, and texts such as these are useful places to start. You could, perhaps, consider the balance between simile and metaphor in a text or part of a text; or how metaphor is used to construct character, either by the narrator, through description, or by characters themselves and their dialogue. Rock and pop song lyrics are another good source of data. Their metaphors may be one-off creative metaphors, or clichéd; they may exploit and develop conventional metaphors or idioms; or whole songs may represent a single, extended metaphor, or realize conceptual metaphors such as LIFE IS A JOURNEY, LOVE IS HEAT, and so on. Consider, for example, classic songs such as The Beatles' 'Yesterday', Bob Dylan's 'Like a Rolling Stone', and the Doors' 'Light my Fire', as well as more recent songs or rap lyrics. We did not really cover serious literature in Chapter 8, although we have quoted from poetry: you could, of course, choose a poem or classic literary text to explore.

Finally, we looked in Chapter 9 at non-verbal metaphor, and commented that we only had space to consider a few contexts such as film, music, art, signs, and statues. To keep investigations simple, start by looking at a single painting (perhaps representational rather than abstract), and see how its meaning is constructed through symbol and metaphor; or look at a photograph in relation to metonymy and metaphor. We have already mentioned non-verbal metaphor in advertising. Another possibility is to explore how newspaper cartoons use metaphor to satirize, or how editors use photographs to comment on as well as illustrate the news. Compare the kinds of image which accompany news reports on television: are they simply informative, or do they have other functions? How far, in fact, do the metaphors explain or evaluate, or do they simply entertain?

See Cameron and Low (1999) for a collection of papers which discuss methodologies in metaphor research in a variety of fields, along with results of investigations.

BIBLIOGRAPHY

Aitchison, J. (2002) *Words in the Mind: an Introduction to the Mental Lexicon*, 3rd edn, Oxford: Blackwell.

Baker, M. (1992) *In Other Words*, London: Routledge.

Black, M. (1993) 'More about metaphor', in A. Ortony (ed.) *Metaphor and Thought*, 2nd edn, Cambridge: Cambridge University Press: 19–41.

Bolinger, D. (1980) *Language – the Loaded Weapon*, London: Longman.

Caballero, R. (2003) 'Metaphor and genre: the presence and role of metaphor in the building review', *Applied Linguistics* 24/2: 145–167.

Cameron, L. (2003) *Metaphor in Educational Discourse*, London and New York: Continuum.

Cameron, L. and Low, G. (eds) (1999) *Researching and Applying Metaphor*, Cambridge: Cambridge University Press.

Carpenter, H. (1985) *Secret Gardens: a Study of the Golden Age of Children's Literature*, London: Allen and Unwin.

Carter, R. (1998) *Vocabulary: Applied Linguistic Perspectives*, 2nd edn, London: Routledge.

—— (2004) *Language and Creativity: the Art of Common Talk*, London: Routledge.

Carter, R. and Nash, W. (1990) *Seeing through Language: a Guide to Styles of English Writing*, Oxford: Blackwell.

Chantrell, G. (ed.) (2002) *The Oxford Dictionary of Word Histories*, Oxford: Oxford University Press.

Charteris-Black, J. (2004) *Politicians and Rhetoric: the Persuasive Power of Metaphor*, Basingstoke: Palgrave.

Cook, G. (1992) *The Discourse of Advertising*, London: Routledge.

Coulthard, M. (1995) 'Explorations in applied linguistics 3: forensic stylistics', in G. Cook and B. Seidlhofer (eds) *Principle and Practice in Applied Linguistics: Studies in Honour of H.G. Widdowson*, Oxford: Oxford University Press: 229–243.

Crisp, P. (2003) 'Conceptual metaphor and its expressions', in J. Gavins and G. Steen (eds) *Cognitive Poetics in Practice*, London: Routledge: 99–113.

Deignan, A. (1995) *Collins Cobuild English Guides 7: Metaphor*, London and Glasgow: HarperCollins.

—— (2005) *Metaphor and Corpus Linguistics*, Amsterdam: John Benjamins.

Fairclough, N. (1989) *Language and Power*, London: Longman.

Forceville, C. (1998) *Pictorial Metaphor in Advertising*, London: Routledge.

Forty, A. (2000; paperback edn 2004) *Words and Buildings: A Vocabulary of Modern Architecture*, London: Thames and Hudson.

Gardner, M. (ed.) (1970) *The Annotated Alice*, revised edn, Harmondsworth: Penguin.

Gavins, J. and Steen, G. (eds) (2003) *Cognitive Poetics in Practice*, London: Routledge.

Gay, P. (1998) 'Origins of the flag in the French Republic'. Online. Available HTTP: <http://flagspot.net/flags/fr.html> (accessed December 2004).

Gibbs, R.W. (1994) *The Poetics of Mind: Figurative Thought, Language, and Understanding*, Cambridge: Cambridge University Press.

Gibbs, R.W. and Steen, G. (eds) (1999) *Metaphor in Cognitive Linguistics*, Amsterdam: John Benjamins.

Goatly, A. (1997) *The Language of Metaphors*, London: Routledge.

Grady, J., Oakley, T. and Coulson, S. (1999) 'Blending and metaphor', in R.W. Gibbs and G. Steen (eds) *Metaphor in Cognitive Linguistics*, Amsterdam: John Benjamins: 104–124.

Halliday, M.A.K. (1994) *An Introduction to Functional Grammar*, 2nd edn, London: Edward Arnold.

Harrison, J. (1996) *Articles indéfinis* (album cover notes), Montréal: empreintes DIGITALes.

—— (2002) *Hot Air*. Online. Available HTTP: <http://www.music.ed.ac.uk/sound/hotair.html> (accessed January 2005).

Jakobson, R. (1960) 'Linguistics and poetics', in T. Sebeok (ed.) *Style and Language*, Cambridge, Massachusetts: MIT Press: 350–377.

Kittay, E.F. (1987) *Metaphor: its Cognitive Force and Linguistic Structure*, Oxford: Clarendon Press.

Kövecses, Z. (2000) *Metaphor and Emotion: Language, Culture and Body in Human Feeling*, Cambridge: Cambridge University Press.

—— (2002) *Metaphor: a Practical Introduction*, Oxford: Oxford University Press.

Kress, G. and van Leeuwen, T. (1996) *Reading Images. The Grammar of Visual Design*, London: Routledge.

Labov, W. (1972) *Language in the Inner City: Studies in the Black English Vernacular*, Oxford: Blackwell.

Lakoff, G. (1987) *Women, Fire, and Dangerous Things*, Chicago: University of Chicago Press.

—— (1993) 'The contemporary theory of metaphor', in A. Ortony (ed.) *Metaphor and Thought*, 2nd edn, Cambridge: Cambridge University Press: 202–251.

Lakoff, G. and Johnson, M. (1980; new edn 2003) *Metaphors we Live by*, Chicago: University of Chicago Press.

—— (1999) *Philosophy in the Flesh: the Embodied Mind and its Challenge to Western Thought*, New York: Basic Books.

Lakoff, G. and Turner, M. (1989) *More than Cool Reason: a Field Guide to Poetic Metaphor*, Chicago: University of Chicago Press.

Lodge, D. (1977) *The Modes of Modern Writing: Metaphor, Metonymy, and the Typology of Modern Literature*, London: Edward Arnold.

McGuinness, H. (1998) Untitled, unpublished manuscript, University of Birmingham.

Mahon, J.E. (1999) 'Getting your sources right: what Aristotle *didn't* say', in L. Cameron and G. Low (eds) *Researching and Applying Metaphor*, Cambridge: Cambridge University Press: 69–80.

Martin, J.R. (1985) *Factual Writing: Exploring and Challenging Social Reality*, Victoria, Australia: Deakin University Press; republished (1989) Oxford: Oxford University Press.

Montgomery, M. (1995) *An Introduction to Language and Society*, 2nd edn, London: Routledge.

Montgomery, S.L. (1991) 'Codes and combat in biomedical discourse', *Science as Culture*, 2 (3), 341–391.

Newmark, P. (1988) *A Textbook of Translation*, London: Prentice Hall.

Ortony, A. (ed.) (1993) *Metaphor and Thought*, 2nd edn, Cambridge: Cambridge University Press.

Oxford English Dictionary (OED) (1989) 2nd edn, Oxford: Oxford University Press. Online, 3rd edn. Available HTTP: <http://www.oed.com> (accessed May 2005).

Pyles, T. and Algeo, J. (1993) *The Origins and Development of the English Language*, 4th edn, Fort Worth, Texas: Harcourt Brace Jovanovich.

Reddy, M.J. (1993) 'The conduit metaphor: a case of frame conflict in our language about language', in A. Ortony (ed.) *Metaphor and Thought*, 2nd edn, Cambridge: Cambridge University Press: 164–201.

Searle, J.R. (1993) 'Metaphor', in A. Ortony (ed.) *Metaphor and Thought*, 2nd edn, Cambridge: Cambridge University Press: 83–111.

Sperber, D. and Wilson, D. (1986) 'Loose talk', *Proceedings of the Aristotelian Society* 86 (1985–1986), 153–171.

—— (1995) *Relevance: Communication and Cognition*, 2nd edn, Oxford: Blackwell.

Stockwell, P. (2002) *Cognitive Poetics: an Introduction*, London: Routledge.

Vestergaard, T. and Schrøder, K. (1985) *The Language of Advertising*, Oxford: Blackwell.

Whorf, B.L. (1956) *Language, Thought, and Reality*, Cambridge, Massachusetts: MIT Press.

Winner, E. (1988) *The Point of Words: Children's Understanding of Metaphor and Irony*, London and Cambridge, Massachusetts: Harvard University Press.

SOURCES FOR TEXTS

CORPUS DATA

The Bank of English (BoE), The University of Birmingham.

NEWSPAPERS AND PERIODICALS

Daily Express, 15 October 2002.

Daily Mail, 25 October 2002, 7 February 2003.

The Guardian, 17 March 2001, 5 October 2002, 25 October 2002, 2 February 2003, 22 November 2003, 10 January 2004, 17 January 2004, 6 March 2004.

The Independent, 14 June 2004.

The Observer, 2 February 2003, June 2003, 23 November 2003, 11 July 2004.

Red, March 2003.

NOVELS AND POETRY

Achebe, Chinua (1958) *Things Fall Apart*; republished (2001), Harmondsworth: Penguin.

Atwood, Margaret (2000) *The Blind Assassin*, London: Bloomsbury.

Auden, W.H. (1966) *Collected Shorter Poems 1927–1957*, London: Faber and Faber.

Bawden, Nina (1973) *Carrie's War*, Harmondsworth: Puffin/Penguin.

Bryers, Paul (2004) *The Used Women's Book Club*, London: Bloomsbury.

Carroll, Lewis (1865) *Alice's Adventures in Wonderland*; republished in M. Gardner (ed.) (1970) *The Annotated Alice*, Harmondsworth: Penguin.

—— (1871) *Through the Looking Glass*; republished in M. Gardner (ed.) (1970) *The Annotated Alice*, Harmondsworth: Penguin.

Grahame, Kenneth (1908) *The Wind in the Willows*; republished (1951), London: Methuen.

Haddon, Mark (2003) *The Curious Incident of the Dog in the Night-time*, London: Random House.

Heaney, Seamus (1998) *Opened Ground: Poems 1966–1996*, London: Faber and Faber.

—— (trans.) (1999) *Beowulf*, London: Faber and Faber.

Joyce, James (1939; 3rd edn 1964) *Finnegans Wake*, London: Faber and Faber.

Lewis, C.S. (1950) *The Lion, the Witch and the Wardrobe*; republished (1988), London: Lions, HarperCollins.

Lorca, Federico García (1992) *Selected Poems*, trans. M. Williams, Newcastle upon Tyne: Bloodaxe Books.

MacDonald, George (1883) *The Princess and Curdie*; republished in R. McGillis (ed.) (1990) *George MacDonald: The Princess and the Goblin and The Princess and Curdie*, Oxford and New York: Oxford University Press.

Morrall, Clare (2003) *Astonishing Splashes of Colour*, Birmingham: Tindal Street Press.

Muldoon, Paul (1996) *New Selected Poems 1968–1994*, London: Faber and Faber.

Ní Chuilleanáin, Eiléan (1986) *The Second Voyage*, Dublin: Gallery Books, and Newcastle upon Tyne: Bloodaxe Books.

Owen, Wilfred (1963) *The Collected Poems of Wilfred Owen*, ed. C. Day Lewis; London: Chatto and Windus.

Rankin, Ian (2003) *Beggars Banquet*, London: Orion.

Tolkien, J.R.R. (1954) *The Two Towers*; republished in (1993) *The Lord of the Rings*, London: HarperCollins.

Tucker, Charlotte M. (1858) *The Green Velvet Dress*; republished in J. Mark (ed.) (1993) *The Oxford Book of Children's Stories*, Oxford: Oxford University Press.

Vine, Barbara (1998) *The Chimney Sweeper's Boy*, London: Viking.

Yeats, W.B. (1950, 2nd edn) *Collected Poems*, London: Macmillan.

OTHER TEXTS

Fantoni, B. (ed.) (2004) *Colemanballs 12*, London: Private Eye.

Greenwood, M., Connolly, M. and Wallis, G. (1999) *The Rough Guide to Ireland*, London: The Rough Guides.

Naughtie, J. (2001) *The Rivals: The Intimate Story of a Political Marriage*, London: Fourth Estate.

INDEX

Capitalized words in the index indicate metaphorical concepts; italics are used to indicate words and phrases discussed, and titles.

eBooks – at www.eBookstore.tandf.co.uk

A library at your fingertips!

eBooks are electronic versions of printed books. You can store them on your PC/laptop or browse them online.

They have advantages for anyone needing rapid access to a wide variety of published, copyright information.

eBooks can help your research by enabling you to bookmark chapters, annotate text and use instant searches to find specific words or phrases. Several eBook files would fit on even a small laptop or PDA.

NEW: Save money by eSubscribing: cheap, online access to any eBook for as long as you need it.

Annual subscription packages

We now offer special low-cost bulk subscriptions to packages of eBooks in certain subject areas. These are available to libraries or to individuals.

For more information please contact webmaster.ebooks@tandf.co.uk

We're continually developing the eBook concept, so keep up to date by visiting the website.

www.eBookstore.tandf.co.uk